HAZELDEN

A SPIRITUAL ODYSSEY

HAZELDEN

A SPIRITUAL ODYSSEY

Damian McElrath, Ph.D.

First published September, 1987.

ISBN: 0-89486-451-3

Library of Congress Catalog Card Number: 87-80566

Printed in the United States of America.

Contents

Preface   1
Introduction   5

1.   The Genesis of an Idea   11

2.   The Beginnings   23

3.   The Program — Keep It Simple   39

4.   Enter the Butlers — The Corporate Culture   51

5.   Fellowship Club   59

6.   The Willmar Connection   69

7.   The Bridge from Willmar to Hazelden   83

8.   A Decade of Growth — 1952-1961   93

9.   Dia Linn — Arboretum and Laboratory   107

10.   The Changing of the Guard   117

11.   The Years of Communal Genius   129

12.   The Culmination of an Idea   143

13.   A Spiritual Odyssey   149

14.   A Continuing Spiritual Odyssey   157

Select Bibliography   167
Index   171

Acknowledgments

Hazelden Educational Materials gratefully acknowledges Midwest Editions for its contribution toward the production of this book and its continuing support to the Hazelden Foundation.

Editors .... Judy Delaney, Don Freeman
Artist .... David Spohn

The author wishes to acknowledge everyone who helped make this book a reality, especially his wife Sandy, whose patience and support brought this venture to a safe harbor.

Preface

WHEN I ARRIVED at Hazelden in 1977 as a Clinical Pastoral Education trainee, I was struck by the power that Hazelden had for radically changing the course of people's lives. Indeed, my personal spiritual journey had come to a halt without my being aware of it, and my association with Hazelden has allowed me to rediscover and re-create my own spiritual odyssey. My perspective of Hazelden over the past decade permits me to view the institution, its people, and its accomplishments as a nineteenth century writer might have called "an unfolding." I see the history of Hazelden as a continuing journey, historical in design and structure, but spiritual in its purpose and accomplishments. I view Hazelden's unfolding as a journey still unfinished. I hope the following pages will justify my title calling Hazelden itself a spiritual odyssey, and that its history is simply a testimony to that.

The written history of Hazelden has been attempted many times before this. Previous writers who had been assigned to or who were volunteers for the task found it unmanageable, surrendered, and turned it over to a future author. There were good reasons why the early attempts did not meet with success. One reason was that clear guidelines as to what type of history or publication Hazelden sought had never been established. Perhaps this was a prudent omission, with management simply trusting a process beyond its control or understanding.

There had been suggestions for a pamphlet for alumni and departing patients; or perhaps a trade book for the public, presenting the entire history of alcoholism treatment in Minnesota and the intimate role Hazelden had played in it. Other suggestions included publishing a pamphlet which would praise and promote the type of health care Hazelden provided; or finally, a direct and honest account, no holds barred — a realistic picture which would present a lively, accurate, readable, and saleable publication.

Another reason the history remained an unfinished and discouraging onus is that the task was viewed as merely a part-time project. At one point someone suggested hiring a professional researcher who could pursue the living tradition, as well as the Hazelden archives, on a full-time basis.

Before coming to Hazelden, I had researched, written, and published a great deal as a professional historian. I expressed my interest in authoring the history of Hazelden some time in 1980. I knew my approach, in order to be successful, would have to be different from previous attempts. I got my opportunity to test a different approach with Hazelden's celebration of the 25th anniversary of Dia Linn, Hazelden's all-women's rehabilitation unit. I decided to write a pamphlet to commemorate the event. As I conceived it then, the pamphlet might serve as a model for a number of historical essays, a series of vignettes, which together could comprise a chronological sequence of reflections on Hazelden's history.

While not too many people took notice of *The Roses of Dia Linn*, it served my purposes well. I was able to go beyond the mere collection of data, and investigate and explore some of the inner dynamics of what Hazelden represents — the development of a brilliant idea in the rehabilitation of chemically dependent people.

I readily and easily came to the conclusion that the history of Hazelden could not be simply a chronological record of data, but rather a description of the dramatic revolution that occurred in the treatment of alcoholics — the genesis of ideas and the genius of the people involved, the tensions among the leadership, and the agony and ecstasy that accompanied developments at every critical juncture. The writing of *Dia Linn* convinced me there were some marvelous things to be told about the emergence and evolution of the Hazelden event.

When I finished the pamphlet, I knew what I could and wanted to do. I desired first of all to avoid the obvious pitfalls involved in writing the history of a remarkably robust and vibrant institution only 35 years young and still growing. The most obvious mistake would be to attempt to collect and collate all the data available. While written history was scarce, oral tradition was alive and superabundant. Hazelden had thousands of living alumni. How many of them should be selected for interviews? What would be a demographically or chronologically representative sample? What might be one historian's dream would have been my nightmare.

Rather than concentrate on a finished scientific history, I decided to generate some sequential reflections upon the history of Hazelden — an essay upon the history of ideas generated by events that could be verified. These events and ideas are interwoven by necessity. The following pages are not intended for the historian of detail but for the inquisitive intellect in pursuit of some of the happenings surrounding the magnificent idea and event that Hazelden represents.

Hazelden's history is full of dialogue and dialectic — the tension between two interacting forces or elements. For example, Hazelden's evolution reflects the successful attempt to bridge the chasm that separates the professional and the layperson in the rehabilitation of the alcoholic. At Hazelden seemingly irreconcilable elements were reconciled into a multidisciplinary approach, one of the essential ingredients in the Minnesota Model of treatment. The dialectic between spirit and structure, the recovering alcoholic and the nonalcoholic, between freedom and discipline, between change and continuity, between the new and the traditional, all find expression in the events that envelop Hazelden.

In reconstructing the past, the following pages seek to represent Hazelden's genesis and evolution; present insights into the actions and ideas of the key people who contributed to its internal and external growth; and explore the spirit and structure, the mystery that underlies the phenomenon of Hazelden.

Over 1600 years ago, the saintly Ambrose said there is no greater obligation than that of giving thanks. I do not intend to single out any person, living or deceased, for special thanks. Anonymity is a singular blessing. I want to thank everyone who assisted in making this book a reality. For those who are not mentioned in the following pages, but who are indeed a part of Hazelden's history, this book is a tribute to them also. I wish I could have mentioned everyone in the text; but if I had done so, this volume would never have emerged in the seven years I spent writing it. This has been a labor of love for me, based upon the impact that Hazelden has had on my life.

Introduction

THE TWO most frequently asked questions about Hazelden can be framed very simply. What does Hazelden do? How did this huge complex emerge in the middle of nowhere?

What Hazelden does it does well in whatever part of its mission it is fulfilling. Officially stated, Hazelden's mission is to provide quality rehabilitation, education, and professional services in chemical dependency and related areas involving addictive behaviors.

Not everyone with the least knowledge of or association with Hazelden is familiar with its corporate mission statement. But they do know Hazelden is a *graceful* place, full of *gracious* people, and a never ending flow of *grateful* patients and pilgrims.

Graciousness is what Hazelden is all about.

Hazelden graces people by standing, with its staff and alumni, as a powerful paradigm of personal service through its continuum and components of rehabilitative care. Hazelden possesses both the existential power of providing services to humankind, and the derivative capacity of setting an example for people to follow. "See, what I have done, you can too." "Witness, what we have dared, you can dare."

Another way Hazelden graces people is through the power of its written and spoken word, namely its Educational Materials Division.

Finally, Hazelden graces people through the power of its tradition, that is, the capacity and ability it has, through training and education, of passing on the rich message it has discovered.

Just as the buildings grace the Hazelden campus with effortless beauty, so Hazelden has graced thousands of people, encouraging, enobling, and enabling them, as well as reminding them of, and representing for them, their dignity and self-worth.

The roots and potential for the Hazelden event are to be found in its historical and unfolding past which indeed can be described as a spiritual odyssey.

Hazelden is located in Center City, Minnesota, about forty-five miles north of the Twin Cities, Minneapolis-St. Paul. Center City's highway sign tells us its population is 400, about half the total number employed by its famous resident, Hazelden. East of Center City on Highway 8 is the entrance to Hazelden. If not for the blue water tower with the name Hazelden emblazoned in blue letters, one could easily pass by the secluded facility. As one turns off of Highway 8 and onto Pleasant Valley Road, immediately visible straight ahead is the Richmond Walker Center, the headquarters of Hazelden's Educational Materials publishing division.

The mile-long drive to the main campus is landscaped on both sides by thousands of beautiful pines planted some 30 years ago. At the end of the drive is a complex of buildings beautifully blended with each other. These, combined with Richmond Walker, probably exceed in square footage all the buildings in downtown Center City. As people view the Hazelden panorama, the question arises, what is the history and meaning of all of this?

The true extent of the activities represented by the attractive buildings is largely unknown by most people, though the Hazelden name is readily identified with chemical dependency. Even those who are involved in some limited way are usually not aware of how wide is the scope of Hazelden's activities.

Part of Hazelden's philosophy is found in the phrase, "Hazelden — always, the pioneer." Hazelden's beginnings were indeed modest, though it soon became a pioneer in developing a rehabilitation model. From there, Hazelden's growth has been spectacular. Today, Hazelden is a pioneer in areas of education, and health promotion, as well as rehabilitation.

Symbolic of Hazelden's mission were three building projects which occurred in the early 1980s. In particular, the Renewal Center, the Richmond Walker Center, and the Cork Center capture in succinct fashion Hazelden's continuing past, present, and potential future.

Recovery begins with the primary rehabilitation program, which has been one of the principal directions of the Hazelden mission since 1949. The seemingly sophisticated and elaborate complex of rehabilitation units had simple beginnings. The original country estate, Hazelden, known to many as the Old Lodge, was purchased to serve as a retreat, a tranquil atmosphere and beautiful environment to begin the road to recovery. Within twenty years, Hazelden had not only expanded physically but had developed into a sophisticated and internationally recognized treatment center.

Ongoing recovery requires renewal. Thus the Renewal Center, which represents the opportunity and place for the recovering person and significant others to internalize the program and process of A.A. and Al-Anon. The Renewal Center serves as a fitting symbol of the addict's potential as a human being on a personal and spiritual journey. The Renewal Center building, located near the lake at the southeastern part of the main campus, is the culmination of the rehabilitation complex.

At the other end of the Hazelden property, to the south of the entrance to the driveway, stands the beautiful Richmond Walker Center, erected in 1985 to respond to the expansion needs of Hazelden's educational mission. The Walker Center is a tribute to the special creativity emerging from Hazelden's mission to educate others through publishing and disseminating the best ideas in the field of chemical dependency, whether these ideas emanate from within or outside of Hazelden. Hazelden truly is a pioneer in its educational commitment. The Educational Materials Division's horizons have extended beyond the field of chemical dependency; its products now deal with a rich variety of problems and responses within the field of chronic illness.

The Walker Center at one end of the campus and the rehabilitation village at the other are not only symbolic of Hazelden's mission but are the two largest revenue producers for this not-for-profit foundation. The Rehabilitation Division continues to do what it does best: restores people's lives through a unique recovery model. The Educational Materials Division serves a larger population. Its publications — books, pamphlets, tapes, films, and audiovisuals — serve the total Hazelden mission, educating both professionals and nonprofessionals, nurturing and nourishing both recovering and nonrecovering people as they continue their own spiritual odysseys.

Early on, the tradition of reading the Big Book, *Alcoholics Anonymous*, became a part of Hazelden's treatment process. This tradition became known as "bibliotherapy," using reading materials that serve as therapeutic tools to help nurture the lifelong process of recovery. The concept of bibliotherapy has become an accepted and important part of recovery programs throughout the world. This is simply an extension of the idea of one alcoholic talking to another over a cup of coffee. Sharing through literature and tapes provides sustenance and enrichment for the recovering chemically dependent person.

Whereas rehabilitation and education have deep roots and long traditions within the Hazelden event, the Cork Center is a relative newcomer. A mammoth building, Cork — a gift to the Hazelden Foundation by Joan Kroc, owner of the San Diego Padres baseball team and widow of Ray Kroc — contains a variety of recreational and training facilities and houses the Health Promotion and Prevention Division as well as the Counselor Training and Continuing Education Division.

In their totality, these three relatively new buildings — the Renewal Center, Richmond Walker, and Cork — represent a global outreach to people in need — the individual, the family, or society at large, whether at home or in the workplace.

At the end of 1949 there was one person being treated at Hazelden. Today there are literally millions of people being assisted through the wide array of services Hazelden offers — rehabilitation, family care, publications, training and continuing education, research and evaluation, consultation, and employee assistance. All of these services fulfill the Hazelden mission and heighten the public's awareness of the power of addiction, the powerlessness of addicted individuals, and the power of the A.A. program and process.

But magnificent buildings and explosive growth cannot describe all that occurred during Hazelden's development. Neither brick and mortar nor Hazelden's wide variety of services is the most eloquent witness to the significant phenomenon that is Hazelden. The following pages seek to explore the deeper reasons for Hazelden's success in helping so many people by providing them direction for their *individual odysseys*.

In the beginning was A.A.
and before A.A. there
was nothing. . . .

1. The Genesis of an Idea

THE HISTORY of Hazelden begins, as does just about everything else associated with Alcoholics Anonymous in Minnesota and the Midwest, with B. Patrick Cronin.

B. Patrick Cronin (1897-1965), whose drinking had cost him job after job, had become a full-fledged alcoholic by age 36. Then in the early summer of 1940, he read a review of the Big Book, *Alcoholics Anonymous,* published in 1939. In seeking help for his drinking problem, Cronin wrote to the General Service Office of Alcoholics Anonymous in New York, inquiring whether Minneapolis had any A.A. members. He received a negative response with the suggestion that he could contact the strong A.A. fellowship in Chicago. Eventually, two Chicago natives to whom his name had been given "barged in" on him on 9 November 1940. The catastrophic Black Blizzard of 1940 began the next day, delaying their departure and providing them with four days to "work on" Cronin. Cronin's dry date was 11 November 1940. Ever since that time, the grateful Cronin's influence on the growth of A.A. throughout the Midwest was preeminent — approximately 450 A.A. groups trace their establishment to his direct or indirect influence.

Cronin's relationship to the beginnings of Hazelden came about indirectly. Of the many thousands that Cronin helped, one was a Catholic priest, Father M., who had lost one religious assignment after another as a result of his drinking. The priest had struggled with a drinking problem for fifteen years. He sincerely thought he could overcome his weakness through willpower. "However, there was a fake premise in my logic inasfar as I maintained the conviction that I would someday become a controlled drinker."

He had been in and out of treatment centers for a cure — one of these was Willmar State Hospital in Willmar, Minnesota in 1942, which Father M. referred to as a "swill hole." This lack of success together with his drinking behavior led to legal proceedings against the priest to have him dismissed from his religious order and suspended from the priesthood.

When he decided to leave his monastery in 1945, Father M. reconstructed the series of events in this way:

> The drinking spree that followed my departure ended in Minneapolis, [leaving me] a near derelict. There my name was given to Pat Cronin, who introduced me into A.A. at the "2218" clubhouse [2218 First Avenue South, the Minneapolis A.A. headquarters].

Father M. recalled it was Cronin who introduced him to Austin Ripley, another recovering alcoholic.

Ripley was a prominent newspaper writer and the famous author of *Minute Mysteries* and *Photo Crimes*. He was a convert to Roman Catholicism and had joined A.A. in Eau Claire, Wisconsin. Father M. was only one in a long line of alcoholic priests both in Minnesota and Wisconsin whom Ripley had been and would be asked to help. These personal experiences motivated him to do something about the plight of the alcoholic clergy. On one occasion he wrote to Archbishop John Gregory Murray of St. Paul:

> In St. Louis a few weeks ago I talked with a priest who now sells furniture in a large department store. He told me of a brilliant alcoholic Jesuit who is timekeeper at a nearby construction project. I know of one alcoholic priest who drives a Chicago streetcar, another one who is a linoleum salesman, and one who is on a Ford production line.

It appeared shameful enough at that time to be a human being and an alcoholic. Doubly shameful was it to be a human being, a priest, and an alcoholic.

After Ripley had become acquainted with Father M. and the difficulties of alcoholic priests, he volunteered assistance in two areas.

1. He spoke to Lynn Carroll, a lawyer and recovering alcoholic, about avenues of recourse the priest might take in the ecclesiastical trial.

2. He offered to talk with Archbishop Murray about diocesan posts should Father M. decide to leave his religious order and be incorporated into the St. Paul archdiocese.

As early as 1945 Ripley felt that Murray could be a central figure and ally in the struggle against alcoholism. He hoped Murray would bring the A.A. movement before the annual Bishops' Meeting in November. Ripley said:

> This matter of alcoholism should be brought into the open, its causes understood, and the stigma removed. There is a vast job to be done in educating the clergy and [Catholic] hierarchy — and it should be under way without further delay.

But for Ripley the immediate need was to offer concrete assistance to the alcoholic priest.

The concept of a treatment center for priests was born in the year 1947, when Lynn Carroll, and Robert McGarvey, a prominent Minneapolis businessman and owner of McGarvey's Coffee, visited Ripley at his home in Colfax, Wisconsin. They wanted a rehabilitation center for all professionals including clergy. Ripley wanted a center exclusively for clergy, especially Catholic clergy. Ripley prevailed for the time being, and a clerical facility became the goal. Archbishop Murray, grateful for Ripley's assistance "in reconstructing several of our priests through the instrumentality of Alcoholics Anonymous in the Twin Cities," pledged an initial $5,000. He also promised his personal recommendation to prominent members of the Catholic hierarchy throughout the United States.

Immediately Ripley and Father M. began to investigate suitable sites for the center — among them a golf course in the Twin Cities and Eaton's Horse Ranch outside Minneapolis — but nothing came of these investigations. Moreover, Father M.'s continual relapses and difficulties with his religious order did not allow him the time and energy for the project. Subsequently, four people emerged as the principal participants in the tentative strategy for a treatment center: Ripley was the master strategist; his chief lieutenants were McGarvey, Carroll, and Jack Kerwin, who was another Minneapolis businessman.

McGarvey, who had a wide circle of Twin Cities contacts, was to promote the local fund-raising. He and Carroll would continue looking for a suitable site. In the meantime, Ripley would tour the East Coast to promote the idea for a treatment facility and solicit support.

McGarvey arranged a dinner at the St. Paul Athletic Club on 12 December 1947 to enlist the aid of wealthy business associates. Contributions and pledges amounted to about $6,000.

McGarvey and Carroll continued to be hesitant about a facility for clergy only, particularly since it would be easier to raise funds for a center dedicated to a much wider clientele. However, Ripley's adamant singleness of purpose and charismatic leadership led McGarvey to believe that Ripley's goal could be accomplished in two phases: a facility for priests first, and then another for other professionals. But the doubts about the wisdom of Ripley's exclusivity persisted and would soon be revived.

At this time, another issue surfaced as Ripley was on his Eastern tour. Given the sublimity of his project, Ripley found it a nuisance to be preoccupied with mundane matters. Consequently, he was hardly amenable to newly appointed business manager Lynn Carroll's suggestion that some restrictions be placed on the use of funds. "But I do not want and will not be agreeable to any arrangement whereby I must 'ask' a treasurer for money with which to execute plans of purpose," Ripley wrote to McGarvey.

The larger issue would be accountability. Ripley was an honest man, but lacked the clarity of fiscal purpose and good managerial sense to enable him to establish credit with the world of financial and business reality. This reality contrasted sharply and eventually clashed with his own idealism and visionary zeal. Ripley bridled at McGarvey's and Carroll's suggestions of a better accounting method, and later seethed at the procrastination and lack of enthusiastic response from the banker, Richard C. Lilly, and the St. Paul oil executive and philanthropist, I. A. O'Shaughnessy. In Ripley's eyes, Lilly and O'Shaughnessy could easily have provided financial support and moral encouragement. What Ripley did not understand was that it was partly his attitude toward finances that caused the financiers to drag their feet.

Nevertheless, the successes of the early months of 1948 added to Ripley's enthusiasm. He had already received a gift of $1,000 from Father Joseph Flanagan of Boys Town; and the president of Notre Dame, Father John J. Cavanaugh, had offered him some property on which to build the center. Ripley had a cold reception from Cardinal Spellman of New York who believed an alcoholic priest should remain a problem hidden from the layman. On the other hand, Ripley's visit with Archbishop Richard Cushing of Boston was warm and encouraging but provided no finances.

Moreover, Bill W., who with Dr. Bob was one of the cofounders of Alcoholics Anonymous, cautioned Ripley in a personal letter about expecting too much from the Catholic hierarchy.

While Ripley was promoting the project in the East, McGarvey, Carroll, and Kerwin were still searching for a place to build a

View overlooking South Center Lake

treatment facility and attempting to open other financial doors.

In early March 1948, the three of them visited the Power estate in Center City, Minnesota. McGarvey wrote to Ripley that the estate was a

> swell layout near Lindstrom ... I can't think but what it would be a wonderful start, if you got the Archbishop [Murray] to go along with you on purchasing the property ... and certainly, Rip, you don't want any such thing as an actual hospital or sanatorium anyway. You want it to be more like a beautiful home and regular living quarters — something like that would be a great start. You would have something to talk about and you could probably raise big money quicker.

In the same letter, McGarvey also hinted at where the big money might come from. Arrangements had been made, probably through the graces of Kerwin who knew both Lilly and O'Shaughnessy, for Ripley "to meet with R. C. Lilly and a group from St. Paul at a later date."

In June 1948, Ripley and Carroll accompanied Archbishop Murray on a site visit to the Power estate. They agreed that it was ideally suited to their purposes and Murray put up $1,000 for an option on the beautiful estate.

The meetings and relationship with Lilly and O'Shaughnessy did not go well. Both Lilly and O'Shaughnessy remained conditional in their support, especially since Ripley's plans for converting the Power estate into a recovery center appeared to cost about $500,000. Lilly expressed no interest unless $300,000 of that could be raised prior to his involvement.

Other difficulties emerged during the summer months of 1948. Kerwin accused Ripley of "using" A.A. to advance his own interests. Kerwin's letter was a scathing denunciation, accusing Ripley of intolerance, arrogant thinking, writing with a vituperative pen, and of being abrasive and pharisaical. Kerwin withdrew from the circle. Carroll and McGarvey remained but a few months longer.

Before that happened, however, a brochure entitled *Guest House* had been written by Ripley who substituted Guest House for Talbott Hall as the name for the planned treatment facility on the Power estate. *Guest House* was printed with the assistance of B. H. Ridder, publisher of the *St. Paul Pioneer Dispatch* and *Pioneer Press*. The style was typical Ripley — oratorical and unctuous. Ripley was also the self-proclaimed director of the new venture. Thus, the concept was no longer merely an idea, but an idea in print.

But that was as far as the idea of the Guest House facility progressed. The Ripley circle disintegrated, the financial support was not forthcoming, and Archbishop Murray lost his $1,000.

Both McGarvey and Carroll became convinced that Ripley's vision of the Guest House, as limited only to the Catholic clergy, was much too restrictive. They decided to broaden the scope to include professionals of all classes. McGarvey wrote to Ripley:

> When I discussed this with you a year ago, I told you that we would be much better off to make it on a broader scale. You disagreed with me and said there was only one way to go and that was your way.

Ripley's fury and frustrations toward McGarvey amounted to a six-page letter. His conclusion: "And brother, you sure as hell are wrong, in my opinion, in your 'attitude' toward the Guest House situation."

Even Archbishop Murray changed his view and did not favor a treatment facility for priests only. He wanted it expanded to include other professionals.

Finally, there was the problem of Ripley himself. Narrowly but strongly motivated and personally intense, his grandiose, aggressive and abrasive character, together with his charismatic manner, became too much for his friends and obviously did not sit well with the phlegmatic St. Paul financiers. They were conservative businessmen and bankers of whom accountability was expected. They quite reasonably expected that others give the same accounting. Ripley bristled at this, erroneously concluding that such requests impugned his integrity.

It was Lynn Carroll who initiated the meeting that changed the course of events. He wrote to Lilly at the beginning of November 1948, requesting a meeting to include himself and Lilly, McGarvey, Father M., Kerwin, O'Shaughnessy, Ridder, and Archbishop Murray. He wrote that the project had been delayed because of unworkable ideas. He, Kerwin, McGarvey, and Father M. believed they had put together a workable plan that would eliminate many of the objections surrounding Ripley's goal. They wanted the opportunity to present it to Lilly.

This new plan evolved into Hazelden — a treatment facility for professionals. The expenditure would be only the purchase of the property, and would not include the $500,000 capital accompanying Ripley's vision.

When Ripley heard of the new "workable and intelligent" plan and the meeting with Lilly to which he was not invited, he was furious at what he labelled the "treacherous methods being employed" to change the project. He considered Carroll's letter to Lilly "sanctimonious, grovelling, and fawning." He wrote to McGarvey: "If such attitudes and actions reflect honest attempts to practice our program, God save A.A." Finally he threatened a lawsuit if the name Guest House was used for the facility.

Out of this November meeting and the new plans presented there, Hazelden, not Guest House, was born. Enter R. C. Lilly. Exit Austin Ripley, a person of great vision and a noble cause. Ripley would continue with bulldog ferocity, tenacity, and singleness of purpose despite innumerable setbacks in his mission to open Guest House for alcoholic priests. This was finally realized in Lake Orion, Michigan, and later in Rochester, Minnesota.

A recovery center based simply upon A.A. for priests was somewhat premature. The Catholic church was not ready for a treatment center for priests operated exclusively by lay people. Only a handful of clergy (such as Father Edward Dowling, a friend and supporter of Bill W.) were perceptive enough to see what A.A. could do. Father Dowling stated:

> I suppose it is hard for some Catholics to realize that God

could operate through an organization like A.A. Christ said that He came not to save the just. And the Scriptures' promise of aid to the humble might be a key that would lead (if a key can lead) some people to recognize the new hope that A.A. offers.

A word is in order about A.A. and Catholics and the importance of Archbishop Murray in the support of Hazelden. Readers will have to discern the direction of the paradox for themselves. Despite and maybe even because of its Catholic beginnings, Hazelden managed to opt for and maintain the nonreligious and nondenominational substance of the A.A. program. A.A.'s program was intended not to offend the religious or nonreligious sensibilities of any of its members.

Bill W. had been anxious that the A.A. program not arouse the suspicion of the Catholic church. Ripley appeared to be treading heavily on what Bill W. had perceived to be somewhat turbulent waters. The influences upon Bill W. and Dr. Bob as cofounders of Alcoholics Anonymous were divergent and manifold. One influence they shared in common was the Oxford Group and its principles. Dr. Ernest Kurtz, in his book *Not-God, A History of Alcoholics Anonymous*, has analyzed and summarized the impact of the Oxford Group. On the positive side, Kurtz noted the Oxford Group's informal settings for meetings (house parties) cultivated a sense of intimate fellowship and was readily adopted by recovering alcoholics.

Since members of the Oxford Group adhered to no theological position but to the ethical practices of a truly Christian life, individuals were not required to abandon their own denominational churches and beliefs. Conversion, to the Oxford Group, meant achieving a changed lifestyle by "passage" through a variety of stages. In short, the Oxford Group attempted to live by its own understanding of fundamental Christianity.

In processing the Oxford Group movement and its principles, A.A. totally omitted the concept and person of Jesus in the conversion and recovery process and even translated the concept of God to a "Higher Power" which in the last analysis could be A.A. itself. These modifications together with other refinements and even radical excisions, such as the rejection of absolutes, were made to avoid any religious association, any Oxford Group implication. Thus, according to Kurtz, A.A. "avoided aggressive evangelism, embraced anonymity, and strove to avoid offending anyone who might need its program."

This sensitivity to anyone who needed the program was why A.A. would avoid anything that smacked of religious demands or obligations. Bill W. believed that an association, apparent or real, with the Oxford Group would turn away many Catholics who could use A.A. By 1955, approximately one-third of A.A. was Catholic.

Bill W. deliberately omitted mentioning absolutes. He mistakenly believed the Catholic church had condemned the Oxford Group. He also suspected that Catholics would refrain or be restrained from attendance at A.A. if it was thought to be a religious (Oxford Group) meeting.

That is precisely what happened in Cleveland, Ohio. As A.A. membership spread from Akron, Ohio to Cleveland in 1949, several A.A. members were Roman Catholics, some of whom began to have scruples about the "Protestant religious service" (the A.A. meeting) in Akron. When they approached their parish priest about their concerns he forbade them to attend, as a violation of God's law. This was a principal factor that made Cleveland A.A. members establish their own meetings in Cleveland. Fortunately, Father Vincent Haas, of St. Martin's Parish in Cleveland, helped allay some of the suspicions aroused by the misinformed parish priest.

It was inevitable some of the Catholic hierarchy were concerned about A.A. because of A.A.'s early evolution from the Oxford Group, because of its anonymity, and its use of the phrase Higher Power. Moreover, the suspicious attitudes prevalent among the American (Catholic) hierarchy in the mid-twentieth century militated against the immediate acceptance of a spiritual fellowship such as A.A. And as Ripley noted, it would take time to substitute the notion of alcoholism as a disease for the old attitude that stressed the need for moral character, free will, and perfection to control the "immoderate" drinker, even more so if the "immoderate drinker" was a member of the priesthood.

Archbishop Murray was an outstanding exception to the accepted stand that the problem of alcoholism was simply one of willpower and grace. He believed in the disease concept and saw what others like Father Dowling and Father John Ford (another friend of the A.A. movement) perceived, namely, the possibility of reconciliation between their theology and the reality of alcoholism as an illness characterized by loss of control.

Archbishop Murray was both sensitive and compassionate to alcoholic priests. In his previous position as Chancellor of the Archdiocese of St. Paul, it had been his job to deal with them. That is the principal reason he was so receptive to Ripley's offer to help. He thought highly of both Carroll and Ripley. He supported Hazelden from the beginning both financially and morally. When other members of the hierarchy wrote inquiring about treating alcoholic priests at Center City, Archbishop Murray wrote to the American hierarchy:

> Permission has been given to the Hazelden Foundation located at Center City within the Archdiocese of St. Paul to accept as guests for physical and moral reconstruction any members of the clergy who may be entrusted to the Foundation for treatment of alcoholism.
>
> The experience that I personally have had with the administration in the care of clerical guests warrants my conviction that the institution is ready to make a distinct contribution to the cause to which it is dedicated.
>
> The general manager, Mr. Lynn Carroll, has been working in this field for the past eight years in the City of Minneapolis, and has given every evidence of competence and devotion to a degree that justifies me in commending him to the favorable consideration of those who seek assistance in solving a very important problem.

Whether a quirk of fate or a providential act — it was most beneficial that Hazelden lost its clerical connection and its explicit Catholic, Christian, and religious character. Had it not, it is difficult to envision how Hazelden would have had such great influence and impact on the state, national, and international community as a rehabilitative, educational, prevention, and training model.

*"We admitted we were
powerless . . . our
lives . . . unmanageable."
from Step One*

2. The Beginnings

FOR THE HAZELDEN EVENT to commence its work to assist
alcoholics, the enterprise needed stability and structure, a purpose, a place, people, and a program, no matter how simple and
experimental these parts were. This is what this chapter is about,
the beginning of Hazelden — the first tentative, hesitant, experimental years. Some things were planned, some evolved naturally.
Some things emerged in the face of adversity. The spiritual person
can discern vestiges of a Higher Power, for as we shall see, powerlessness and unmanageability abounded and much evolved
through a Power greater than any individual.

Stability and Structure

Richard Coyle Lilly (1884-1959), whom Lilly Hall at Hazelden is
named for, was a prominent banker and financier in the Upper
Midwest during the first half of the twentieth century. In addition
to his banking career, he was identified with the successful development of many philanthropic organizations in the Minneapolis-
St. Paul area (the Lilly Dry Milk Foundation was formed in 1941,
and the Richard Coyle Lilly Foundation in 1944).

The following story is repeated often enough to be a tradition
and therefore partially true although it does not have the ring of
complete authenticity. Described as a "hard-drinking, hard-
playing, and hard-nosed banker," Lilly was playing poker one
night at the Minnesota Club in St. Paul; on his way home, he
mistook a curve on the St. Paul High Bridge which crossed the
Mississippi River. As the story goes, he forgot to straighten his
wheels, and landed 120 feet below on a sand-laden barge passing
beneath the bridge. No one could understand how he came out

Aerial view of Hazelden — early fifties

alive. This accident precipitated not only the decision on Lilly's part to stop drinking, but led to his awareness of, and interest in, alcohol problems in general.

In 1947 Lilly became interested in establishing a treatment center for alcoholic clergymen of all faiths. As a result of the November 1948 meeting (from which Austin Ripley had been ostracized), the Coyle Foundation authorized the purchase of the Power farm (known as Hazelden), from the Power family for $50,000 on 29 December 1948. The property was worth a great deal more than the initial sale price of $75,000. Archbishop Murray's original investment of $1,000 and his prominence had obviously exercised some impact on the negotiations. His loss proved to be a net gain of $24,000.

The minutes of the 29 December board of trustees meeting of the Coyle Foundation stated:

> The expectation is that this corporation [Coyle Foundation] will, in turn, sell the premises on somewhat similar terms to a charitable hospital corporation about to be formed, probably under the name of Hazelden Foundation. The new hospital corporation is to operate the premises as a sanatorium for curable alcoholics of the professional class.

Less than two weeks later this was accomplished. The Hazelden Foundation was incorporated on 10 January 1949, with its objective, according to the minutes of the Coyle Foundation's board meeting, "to operate a public hospital or hospitals for the purpose of furnishing hospitalization to the sick." Hazelden was (and remains) a not-for-profit corporation. The first meeting of Hazelden's Board of Trustees was held the following day, in St. Paul, at which time the by-laws were adopted. R. C. Lilly became the board's first president; Kerwin, McGarvey, and Carroll were the first vice presidents. A. A. Heckman, a friend of Lilly's, was also a member of the board; T. D. Maier was secretary and treasurer. The Power farm was purchased from the Coyle Foundation for $50,000 under a contract for deed dated 11 February 1949. Carroll was employed as general manager of Hazelden at a salary of $600 per month, plus $35 per month for car allowances and other reasonable expenses.

With the fact of incorporation, a necessary measure of structure and stability was provided the fledgling enterprise.

Purpose

The purpose of the organization had to be more clearly defined.

Ripley's concept of a center for alcoholic priests had been replaced by a center for professional people. Once that had been established, some clarification was necessary regarding the Coyle Foundation's expectation that "the new hospital corporation is to operate the premises as a sanatorium for curable alcoholics of the professional class."

McGarvey undertook the task of expanding upon the purpose for which Hazelden had been formed and defining the clientele it would serve. He did this in a five-page letter in preparation for the spring opening. It was McGarvey's belief the effectiveness of the program would reside in the realization "that one alcoholic understands his fellow alcoholics' problems and they let their hair down to each other and they can really diagnose their case properly and help [each other if everyone] wants to be helped." It was simply a translation of Bill W.'s basic insight that recovery comes about from one alcoholic talking to another over a cup of coffee.

Regarding admissions, McGarvey wrote that all men and women deserve help with alcoholism, but, because of the size of Hazelden, admission would be limited at first to the clergy and professional men. (Women patients were not admitted at Hazelden until 1956, with the opening of Dia Linn in White Bear Lake, Minnesota.) They would be expected to pay, or other means of payment would be found. The hope and the vision of the future was much broader and breathtaking. According to McGarvey:

> As time goes on it is our hope to enlarge on this whole facility so as to help and accept every alcoholic in need and who is deserving so that this institution, or home, will eventually turn out hundreds and thousands of cured, or at least arrested, alcoholic diseased patients. It looks like this is a dream that is finally going to come true, and as time goes on more buildings and more facilities can be added on this large property.

From our vantage point today, McGarvey was quite prophetic.

Place

The following description of the Hazelden manor appeared in the 16 October 1949 edition of the *St. Paul Pioneer Press*:

> The main farmhouse is an attractive, rambling one-and-one-half story structure with white-shingled sides and a red roof. It appears to be a modest dwelling at first glance, but has seventeen spacious rooms, including a large living room

Old Lodge after expansion — 1952

and dining room, a well-stocked library, an attractive sun porch and numerous bedrooms, some of master size.

There are two cottages also, one equipped with indoor recreational facilities, the other close to and overlooking the lake (a bay of South Center Lake). And there is a house in which lives a farmer, who leases a portion of the land for agricultural use and specializes in breeding purebred Hereford cattle.

The main farmhouse became the center of treatment, and remains the only original structure at Hazelden. It is now known as the Old Lodge, and still retains much of its original charm. The grounds then consisted of 217 acres of rolling land, some of which was being cultivated, some remained woodland, with about a mile of lakeshore on South Center Lake.

Before being known as the Power estate, the property on which Hazelden stands was known as the Porter farm, after the late Andrew Porter. Charles Power of North Branch, Minnesota acquired the property in 1925, the same year he married Hazel Thompson of the Thompson family that owned the Pioneer Press Publishing Company. From that year on, the farm was called "Hazel"-den after Power's first wife. The suffix "den" had no particular significance according to Power's son, Charles, except it was a natural elongation of Hazel.

When Ripley appropriated the title, Guest House, and the process of incorporation demanded a title, the board simply used the official letterhead title of the Power farm. Thus the word Hazelden was attached to a rehabilitation setting and perdured to become synonymous with a pioneering attitude, innovative spirit, and a quality of care surpassed by none other in the field of chemical dependency.

People

Besides a place to locate itself, the treatment center required people to care for the patients. Hazelden needed someone to initiate and direct a program, no matter how simple it might be.

After dinner one evening in January 1949, Lilly offered the position to Carroll, who had been the catalyst for the November 1948 meeting at which agreement had been reached about the nature and new direction of the program.

Lynn Bernard Carroll was born 8 July 1898 in Minneapolis. After graduating from high school, he enlisted in the Royal Canadian Flying Corps where he served for eleven months. Upon discharge, he returned to Minneapolis and enrolled in the Minnesota College of Law. He graduated in 1922 and entered private practice, specializing in insurance litigation.

In Carroll's life, personal suffering had lasting significance. An alcoholic, he emerged from near helplessness and despair to devote his life to helping other alcoholics, with profound consequences for himself. In moving from personal calamity to a life of outstanding service, he is a notable example of recovery from alcoholism.

Carroll began to experiment with alcohol in law school; in 1922 he wrote several of his bar examinations in a state of intoxication. Unaware of the signs of incipient alcoholism, he continued to drink heavily for several years without excessive worry.

Inevitably, his drinking bouts grew longer and more frequent. As time confirmed his dependence on alcohol, he began to look for ways to control his drinking. Repeatedly, he took the pledge to abstain; his periods of sobriety dwindled from eleven months to eleven days, and then vanished. He consulted physicians. He began to leave town when he felt the compulsion to drink. Like Father M., he sought a formula for controlled drinking; all the while, his drinking remained in an aggravated, progressive state. His legal practice deteriorated, and in 1938 it disappeared. His family suffered. Finally, on 11 April 1941, he was confined to the psychiatric ward of General Hospital in Minneapolis.

When Carroll emerged from confinement three days later, he sought the fellowship of Alcoholics Anonymous. He subsequently became a member of the original A.A. group in the Minneapolis area. He took his last drink 2 February 1942.

Thereafter, with the empathy and the enthusiasm perhaps only a recovering alcoholic can know, he committed himself to helping other suffering alcoholics. He taught a series of classes at the "2218" Minneapolis A.A. headquarters. Speaking engagements took him all over Minnesota and throughout the Upper Midwest. Within six years he had become a highly respected and well-known figure in A.A. circles.

It was while Carroll and other adherents of A.A. (notably McGarvey whom Carroll sponsored, and Ripley whom Carroll met at "2218") were communicating A.A.'s program to a widening audience of alcoholics, the need for a rehabilitation center for alcoholics emerged. It was because of Carroll's already outstanding work with alcoholics that Lilly offered him the position of director in 1949.

Carroll's position entailed partial responsibility for paying a large debt incurred by purchase of the estate; this was expected to be financed through fund-raising and patient revenue. After talking it over with his wife, Carroll accepted the offer, realizing in his position he could exercise his philosophy of treatment for alcoholism more intensively. For three years he was the only full-time counselor on the staff. In the beginning he lived at Hazelden practically all the time, receiving occasional relief when some A.A. person would be his substitute. His schedule was exhausting, and additional fund-raising efforts were frustrating. But he persevered and served to hold things together during the critical transition from Lilly's hands to the purchase of Hazelden by the Butler family.

Extraordinary as Carroll's career at Hazelden was, the most remarkable aspect of his life was his personal recovery. In rising above the severe limitations imposed by his alcoholism, he was an example of the alcoholic who achieves recovery through application of the principles of Alcoholics Anonymous. This remained the cornerstone of the Hazelden program.

Lynn Carroll   *"Ma" Schnable*

The successes of his career can be considered the credentials of his recovery. He established himself as a foremost proponent of the A.A. philosophy, a lay therapist in the field of alcoholism, and a teacher of other counselors-on-alcoholism. As a leader in the treatment of alcoholics, he was able to enunciate the stages of his own personal growth and self-development.

Carroll was good as both counselor and lecturer. He was dedicated, intelligent, and had a logical and legal mind. Best of all, he knew an alcoholic's needs; and he knew, both cognitively and experientially, the A.A. program. He spoke of himself as an opinionated person, and it will be seen how his convictions and attitudes would conflict with what he called the "professional approach and mentality" in the development of the Hazelden genius and its understanding of treatment.

Initially, Carroll's staff consisted of three other people. The most important was Ma Schnable, a nurse and cook who did everything except formal counseling. Carroll was told about Ann Schnable, "Ma" as she was affectionately known, during the open house days in April 1949. She and her husband had at one time owned a hotel in Taylors Falls, Minnesota, about ten miles northeast of Center City. Her original intention had been to assist with the cooking at the open house, but she stayed ten years. An excellent cook as well as being a registered nurse, she was marvelously compassionate. Nevertheless, nobody was allowed to intrude in her kitchen unless one was willing to risk being run out.

In charge of maintenance was Jimmy Malm, who had been the grounds keeper for the Power family. He elected to stay on as grounds keeper but had nothing to do with the patients.

The final staff person was the utility man. There was a rapid turnover of help in this position. He did a variety of tasks including lifting men back into bed especially during times of withdrawal. There is a story of one patient who kept falling out of bed; the utility man (a position which evolved into the patient care coordinator, and eventually into the unit manager) was getting annoyed at repeatedly lifting the patient and putting him back into bed. He devised a homemade solution. He put a white coat and a stethoscope on another patient whom he coached to pretend to give a medical examination and to say in the hearing of the other patient, "He'll be all right if he lies there absolutely still. Otherwise I can't vouch for him." The other patient did not move for 48 hours. Four or five days later when the new patient was able to focus his eyes and his attention, he recognized the medical pretender as just another patient. He was able to laugh at the trick played on him.

Patients would stay as long as Carroll could urge them. In some instances, the client came in for one night and departed the next day. One guest returned six times in nine months. A fee was required, which was paid through private means, but there was assistance for exceptions. Free care became a strong emphasis at an early stage of Hazelden's history.

Although one person was admitted in April, Hazelden officially opened 1 May 1949. A few months later, Carroll, in a newspaper interview, described Hazelden's purpose:

> Any successful treatment for alcoholism must be based for the most part on psychology. The obsession for alcohol can only be eliminated by clear and natural thinking. Time and patience are required as are understanding, guidance, and helpful companionship.
>
> All this can be best accomplished in a healthful and restful environment such as Hazelden represents. This is not a hospital but a home. Neither is it operated as an institution, in the general sense of the word.
>
> We have no medical staff — only a physician in a nearby town upon whom we may call in case of illness. We have no attendants keeping tab on the men here, because we feel that they are entitled to personal privacy. We have only four em-

ployees, including a cook.

In the life at Hazelden, there is only one restriction — no alcohol — and it is heartening to see the way in which the men live up to it.

Looking back years later after he had departed from Hazelden, Carroll reflected that when the program opened there was no model to follow. He wanted the men to stay three weeks, and to provide them with an environment where, once they were dry, they could be educated to the A.A. program. They needed the time and opportunity to, according to Carroll, "correct some of their character defects — anger, fear, hatred, self-pity — which is the curse of, well, the curse of the human race, not only of the alcoholic." In the last analysis, the point of getting patients to Hazelden was to give them time to learn about A.A. and start to live it. Carroll simply stated, "I know that A.A. work[s]." It was in this tradition Hazelden was to follow and never waver. A.A. became Hazelden's healing reservoir.

In the early months of the new venture, Carroll grappled with the central issue: should he not have some psychological or psychiatric background? According to Carroll:

> There were a lot of problems I hadn't learned to work out quite right. And then I got to think — what the dickens! I had had psychiatrists and psychologists and they didn't do me any good and I didn't know any other alcoholic that they ever did anything for.

He concluded that since he was getting good results, he would continue doing what he did best. He developed a recovery course based on the straight A.A. program and process. He would talk to the patients about the Steps.

It is important to remember part of Carroll's conviction was that the only manner in which an alcoholic could really be helped was through the A.A. Steps and another alcoholic. Carroll would have a difficult time when a nonrecovering psychologist wanted to add the psychological profile of a patient — the MMPI (Minnesota Multiphasic Personality Inventory) — to the treatment process.

This may be simply stated but, as we shall see in the chapters that follow, it is not an oversimplification. Causes of friction between Carroll and Hazelden (for example, the building of large edifices and the payment of modest wages) could not conceal the underlying problem, what Carroll considered the insidious intrusion of psychological principles into the A.A. program.

Contemporary society places great emphasis in the health care system upon the evaluation of outcomes. Chemical dependency is no exception. It is interesting to witness that from the moment Hazelden opened its doors, Lynn Carroll, encouraged by A. A. Heckman, a member of the board of trustees, sought to keep track of the men who had undergone treatment at Hazelden. When Carroll reported to the board in January 1951, he indicated that as of 15 December 1950, 156 men had been to Hazelden. Of the 156 admitted, Carroll wrote that 78 percent had recovered and demonstrated marked progress. These included both those who had not relapsed and those who had relapsed and were recovering. The method of verification was unsophisticated and probably would not survive scientific scrutiny. Nevertheless, according to Carroll:

> Our means of determining and keeping in touch with patients who have left is an excellent one as our A.A. contacts usually report on those men from time to time. This includes men from neighboring states who have been directed to Hazelden by their doctor, or by A.A. contacts. Some of the men as far away as Montana have returned for visits while they are in the city. There are a few, however, whom we have been unable to trace and those number fourteen, or 8.8 percent of the men who have been patients at Hazelden.

Exactly the same number (fourteen) were still drinking. Finally, of the 156 men who had been to Hazelden, three had died and one had gone insane.

Regarding those who relapsed and recovered, Carroll made an interesting observation:

> In some cases there seems to be an inclination to have one experimental drinking bout after leaving Hazelden, but this seemed definitely and finally to decide for the patient that he could never drink again.

There were two further interesting points about Carroll's report. One was the number of repeaters. While the number of men who came to Hazelden during the period was 156, the total number of admissions had been 300. Hazelden was and continues to be a haven for repeaters, especially today when it is often seen as the resource of last resort. In Hazelden's first year and a half, one individual had been admitted fifteen times "not because of relapses," Carroll said, "but in order to avoid relapses." Even then

Hazelden substituted as an aftercare and renewal center.

Of the relapsed, Patrick Butler would be anxious (when the Butler family later assumed control) that Hazelden not become a three- or four-day "soaking pit" or " boiling out operation." Various solutions and remedies would be applied to the treatment of the "revolving door" alcoholic.

The second point of interest in Carroll's report was his comparison of the success ratio between those who were beneficiaries of the Lexington-Hill Grant (Louis W. Hill, railroad magnate and philanthropist) and the self-pay clients. He noted that the men who were supported by the Hill Grant (obtained through the efforts of Lilly and Heckman) stayed four weeks or longer while the others remained an average of two weeks and five days. Carroll reasoned it would "appear that the percentage of recovery is stepped-up considerably when an additional week or two is added to the stay," because recipients had more time to absorb the principles of the program. There was a sense that a longer program was the ideal. Twelve men had been through the program under the auspices of the Lexington-Hill Grant; ten of them were recovered, one relapsed and recovered, and one was still drinking. Carroll remarked upon their cooperation and the fine example they set for others. Since their departure from Hazelden, all except one had been active in A.A.

Vision of the Future

Mention of the Lexington Foundation brings us to A. A. Heckman, who was one of the original incorporators of the Hazelden Foundation. He was responsible in great part for the vision of what Hazelden could be and what it did become as it grew for three decades. Heckman's involvement in Hazelden began with his role as personal friend, consultant, and advisor to R. C. Lilly in philanthropic matters.

When it became clear that some geographical point of administrative contact was necessary in St. Paul, Heckman offered to make his office and secretary at St. Paul Family Service available to Hazelden for this purpose.

On 19 September 1949, the board of Hazelden discussed the need to provide free board to deserving persons who did not have the finances to stay at Hazelden. Lilly suggested this be supported by funds donated by the Lexington Foundation. Heckman was instrumental in obtaining the initial contribution of $5,000 for 1949.

Heckman was genuinely concerned about the nature of the Hazelden effort and the validation of its effectiveness. Very early in his relationship with Hazelden, he wrote a memorandum to Louis W. Hill and reminded him an institution for the treatment of alcoholics was not new. Moreover, treatment results had often been excellent especially when coordinated with good psychiatric and medical care as well as with Alcoholics Anonymous. Heckman clearly saw community benefits from such treatment since alcoholism cost hundreds of thousands of dollars annually to employers and taxpayers.

He was perceptive enough to notice a large volume of cases in municipal court and the workhouse were alcohol-related.

> [In 1949] at least 15 percent of relief cases have alcoholism as a problem, I think. Best figures available indicate St. Paul has at least 3500 excessive drinkers and alcoholics.

In this same memorandum, Heckman raised several issues which he thought had to be addressed if the program were to be successful.

- There was the need for a good, well-rounded board of directors with the medical, religious, and psychiatric professions represented by working members, just as Lilly insisted that level-headed businessmen be on the board to assure sound management.
- It is interesting, again at this very early stage, to see Heckman stating that Alcoholics Anonymous should be a part of the program, but not all of it. He felt A.A. "must not be allowed to 'run away' with this kind of program." This insight ought not to be seen as negative but as an anticipation of a multidisciplinary team or a model of cooperation between the professional and nonprofessional. This was 1949, and Heckman's reflections anticipate the experiment with a multidisciplinary approach that was conducted at Willmar State Hospital under Nelson Bradley in the fifties and was transferred and perfected at Hazelden in the sixties under Daniel Anderson.
- Heckman indicated he had spoken with Lilly about the need to treat all who were treatable regardless of economic, social, or educational background. Prior to Heckman's memorandum, Lilly inclined toward the idea of limiting entrance to the white-collar and professional groups.
- Heckman supported all efforts to work on admission policies and on establishing operating income. He concluded it was difficult to appraise Hazelden so early in its career except to

A. A. Heckman   *Lynn Carroll*   *R. C. Lilly*

say there was great need for such a program.

Heckman was an extremely important asset both when Hazelden opened its doors and during the years of its subsequent history. During Hazelden's first four years, he was instrumental in procuring the Hill Grant which amounted to $20,000 (a substantial sum in those days). He also continually suggested Hazelden measure the effectiveness of its programs and its results.

As the program ended its second year, Heckman wrote:

> In making a judgment of success we must depend to a large extent upon Lynn Carroll's reports and those of the members of A.A. who are active in the work of Hazelden. A good many of the men treated at Hazelden are known to Family Service; thus giving me another source of information.
>
> The records of Family Service and the Ramsey County Probation Office confirm the reports of Lynn Carroll.
>
> However, I believe it would be worthwhile to have an objective evaluation of all patients discharged from Hazelden since it opened its doors. This evaluation should include a follow-up of each discharged patient with an objective appraisal of his adjustment socially, economically, and in relationship to use of alcohol following his treatment at Hazelden. A graduate student in sociology, psychology, or psychiatry at the University of Minnesota might be available for such a study and appraisal.

The seminal idea of a good evaluation system was sown almost

A Spiritual Odyssey

twenty years before it became a reality. In 1970 the Hill family provided a very substantial sum to support research on the individual outcome of Hazelden's treatment program. Again, Heckman was instrumental in procuring this grant.

Two years after the program started, Heckman clearly saw that Hazelden's success was the result of three converging elements: the blending of the philosophy of A.A. with the skills of a lay therapist (Carroll) occurring in a special environment. According to Heckman:

> I think we all agree that the effectiveness of the treatment at Hazelden is due, to a large extent, to the unusual skill of Lynn Carroll. This is fine, except that we do not know to what extent the skills possessed by Carroll can be taught to others. Unless this can be determined, Hazelden faces a big risk and is in a dangerous position should anything happen to Carroll. One always should feel insecure about a program the success of which is dependent solely upon one person.

> If it can be discovered that Carroll's techniques and skills are transmittable to others through teaching and understudying, then steps should be taken to develop several understudies — not only for the sake of Hazelden, but to aid other programs such as Pioneer House [the first A.A.-based treatment center in Minnesota, purchased by Hazelden in 1981] and the program at the state hospital in Willmar.

> It would seem to me that it would be wise to start now trying to develop a research project which would aim to identify those elements in Carroll's skills which can be taught to others. Here again the University of Minnesota might well be the source of such professional research assistance.

Besides encouraging the development of a training component for the benefit of Hazelden and other centers, Heckman continually urged Hazelden to enter into an effective and close day-by-day working relationship with the University of Minnesota's Medical School and Departments of Psychiatry, Psychology, and Sociology. "We had hoped for this in the early planning of Hazelden," Heckman wrote. He looked upon evaluation and training to be areas for university research and collaboration.

Heckman's presence on the board provided it with a vision of professionalism and a strategy for growth and development. He was a most valuable source of ideas, support, and encouragement, and a key figure in the continued development and enlargement of Hazelden's mission as it unfolded.

The Triumvirate

Lilly, Carroll, and Heckman form an essential triumvirate in the early, middle, and contemporary unfolding of Hazelden.

Lilly's participation was short-term, but without him Hazelden would not have had its initial financial viability. In this regard, his contribution was vital, although he withdrew his support several years later.

Carroll's contribution was long-term and substantial. He set the course of Hazelden's treatment program and guaranteed its adherence to a fundamental, philosophical, and pragmatic approach. He had a mission to help alcoholics recover, and he guaranteed Hazelden's participation in that mission at great personal sacrifice.

Initially, Heckman's contribution was much less visible. He was a strategist, futurist, and an idea man who envisioned the enormous potential of Hazelden for people who needed its help. He also envisioned Hazelden as serving as a paradigm for the community at large. During the 36 years that he served on Hazelden's Board of Trustees, he continued to gently remind other board members of Hazelden's need to grow and to change as circumstances and challenges required.

*"Came to believe that a Power greater than ourselves . . ."
from Step Two*

3. The Program — Keep It Simple

AS THE YEARS progressed and Hazelden's program became more sophisticated, some fundamentals were always in place. These fundamentals were intended to implant the A.A. program and process: abstinence, attendance at A.A. meetings (a change of behavior), and familiarity (intimacy) with the Big Book of Alcoholics Anonymous. These program elements simply reinforced Bill W.'s and Dr. Bob's principle of recovery: one alcoholic talking to another over a cup of coffee. This was eminently successful because in its simplicity the A.A. program incorporated and captured fundamental insights into human nature and the human condition.

When Hazelden officially opened its doors on 1 May 1949, the program expectations were few and simple. The patients were expected to:

- practice responsible behavior;
- attend the lectures on the Steps;
- associate and talk with the other patients; and
- make their beds.

These expectations were intended to support the overall goal of remaining abstinent. Obviously there was to be no alcohol on the premises.

In his first report to the directors of Hazelden, Carroll described how A.A. permeated the program.

> A.A. discussions or discussions of any kind are held at the will of the group or the individual. We are deeply indebted to the A.A. groups in Minneapolis and St. Paul for their cooperation in arranging weekly discussion groups at Hazelden. We

The atmosphere of acceptance and fellowship

39

try to have at least one of these meetings each Thursday night of the week.

A.A. people would occasionally stay over allowing Carroll the opportunity to spend a night with his family.

There was a great deal of informality. The administration of the place was loosely structured. Carroll and Ma Schnable distributed the vitamins as well as the medicines prescribed by a doctor; doctor's instructions were always followed and no medications were given without approval. Carroll kept all of the books and the "medical records" — a simple card with some essential biographical data including the days of admission and departure.

The admission process was simple. Patients could be expected at any time of the day or night. Sometimes notice would be given; at other times it was not unusual for A.A. members to drop their more difficult "pigeons" unexpectedly at the door. The method of payment was the assurance: "Oh, he's good for it."

Patients arrived in a variety of ways and in a variety of conditions. One client arrived from Duluth in a hearse. His story is humorous even if all the details cannot be verified. According to Pat Butler:

> He had been in a fleabag hotel up there; and some A.A.'s had gotten ahold of him. Evidently it was hard to convince him that he should go a hundred miles south to Center City and get over his problem. So when he arrived, it was in a hearse, on a stretcher with a blanket on him. When they brought him inside and removed the blanket, he was as naked as a jaybird except for one sock. So I will give you one guess as to what he was called: Chief One Sock, of course.

At the outset, repeaters were common. Some men would come just to dry out. One of the earliest patients who later became Hazelden's second chairman of the board, Patrick Butler, recalled:

> I remember there was one fellow who had a great line of reasoning. He would say: "I won't take another drink; but if I do, I won't get drunk; but if I do, I can always go to Hazelden." One time he called up and we said: "No, we won't take you." He never had a drink after that. He had concluded: "I'm *that* bad that they won't let me in." There's something to that type of rejective treatment.

In the first year, Carroll experimented with an adapted variation of a condition reflex approach for those he felt needed it. He described it to the board as an "aversion treatment," an additional tool

for those attempting to overcome their dependency. It does not in any way provide a permanent solution. This problem rests with the continuation of A.A. It does, however, provide a temporary assistance to those who then may be able to stop their drinking long enough to acquire the philosophy of A.A.

Carroll was not beyond a little deception. He persuaded a patient to submit to the aversion treatment, telling him another patient would do so only if he did. Carroll would then take the second patient aside and issue the same call for help. Carroll's subterfuge was successful. Both patients thought they were assisting Carroll in helping the other and both underwent the aversion treatment — a most unpleasant experience, in which a patient was given such an excess of alcohol that it made him so sick he wouldn't want another drink for a long time — enough time for the A.A. program to sink in.

It was a time of humor and pathos. One patient who could not be persuaded to stay at Hazelden burned to death less than a week after his departure. His davenport caught fire while he was inebriated.

As the population increased and the financial picture brightened, Carroll was permitted the luxury of an assistant counselor. In the early winter of 1951, he asked Otto Zapp, a financier and banker from St. Cloud, Minnesota, if he'd be interested in working at Hazelden a few days each week. Zapp, who had watched, encouraged, and contributed to the Hazelden event from its earliest days, was eager to assist.

Carroll and Zapp worked out an informal arrangement whereby Zapp worked Monday, Tuesday, and Wednesday, and Carroll worked the remaining four days. Chet Burke, a handyman and assistant counselor at Hazelden, had been helping Carroll on alternate weekends since November 1950, and continued to assist after Zapp's arrival. Neither Burke nor Zapp were salaried, although Zapp received expenses to and from St. Cloud. Zapp left Hazelden in January 1953, but during that same month he was contacted by Pat Butler and agreed to return for a salary of $200 per month. He subsequently resumed his duties on the same three-day-per-week schedule, and remained until 1955.

Zapp first met Carroll at an A.A. picnic in August 1945, shortly after he had stopped drinking. He was still uncomfortable in his sobriety. Guests were asked to give their impressions of A.A. Zapp recalled:

> I was seated between two fellows who sobered up in A.A. When it came our turn, they made me stand up. I said this was the pits.

After the testimonials, Zapp felt generally miserable and wandered off alone, wishing for a drink. Carroll approached him and asked if they could talk. As a result, Zapp came away greatly relieved and thereafter relations between the two became very cordial. Zapp reminisced:

> If I had not said what I did, Lynn might not have cornered me, and there's a chance I might still be drunk today.
>
> Once I was having coffee in a restaurant and I overheard Carroll — he must have intended me to hear it — tell some other fellows: "Zapp has A.A. to the nth degree." You see, I couldn't get drunk if he were going around saying that about me to everybody in A.A.

The first time Zapp came to Hazelden as Carroll's assistant, he unsuspectingly walked in the kitchen door and was promptly expelled by Ma Schnable who informed him he had no business there. The rest of his training was a brief encounter with Carroll who "rattled on" about A.A. and did not tell him a thing about Hazelden's program or schedule except to inform him he was to give a talk to the "fellows" at 9:00 the next morning. The essence of Hazelden's first training program was that Zapp ended up pretty much on his own. When he arrived on Monday mornings, Carroll would tell him how far his lectures on the Twelve Steps had progressed, and Zapp would pick up at that point.

Zapp's recollection of his early counseling days provide authentic insights into the nature of the program at its inception. When Zapp came to Hazelden in 1951 the program was essentially what it had been in 1949 and what it would be in 1962. The simple expectations remained constant: lectures, group, and responsible behavior. For its part, Hazelden provided a beautiful, wholesome, and clean environment, excellent food, and an A.A. counselor.

Zapp was not the great speaker Lynn Carroll was. His false teeth impeded his speech. When he went through the ritual of removing his false teeth and putting them in his pocket, he was able to speak with confidence. He was concerned about his speak-

Reading room and library — Old Lodge

ing talent, his effectiveness, and the organization of his short talks. He confided his concerns to Pat Cronin, "Mr. A.A.," who was visiting Hazelden one Sunday. Cronin assured him: "Otto, you know more about it than the patients do, no matter what the hell you tell them." Although there was no formal evaluation of his lectures, Zapp's confidence zoomed after this conversation and he believed the patients seemed satisfied with his fifteen to twenty minute talks. Pat Butler, an excellent speaker himself, remained a staunch advocate of the lecture series and, throughout the years, he sought to strengthen and enhance it in a variety of ways. Although Butler believed thirty minutes was sufficient time to deliver a lecture, Zapp said Butler suggested to him that he lengthen his lectures to forty or fifty minutes. This caused Zapp some anxiety, but that passed in due course.

Zapp initiated an afternoon round-table discussion. All the patients were required to attend and they talked about anything and everything pertaining to alcoholism. Although he tried to be just one of the "fellows" and encouraged dialogue among the patients, the educative process continued, for he had to answer many questions.

Informal "bull sessions" permeated the day, the evening, and the night. They generally occurred over coffee in the kitchen or in the library and sometimes ran into the early hours of the morning. The patients were encouraged to talk among themselves; but the round-table rap sessions with Carroll, Zapp, or Burke as moderators or experts-in-residence were extremely popular and a high point in the program. A.A. meetings or visits by other members of the fellowship were equally welcome. Part of the day was also spent counseling the patients individually but this was never the most important element of the program.

The educative process — brought about intellectually by the lecture and experientially by the bull sessions, the storytelling, and the group with the experts-in-residence — continues to this day, although more formally, as the communicative substance of the Hazelden program. The underlying principle was and still is that recovery takes place with one alcoholic talking to another over a cup of coffee. This principle is based upon the basic human fellowship that, as Ernest Kurtz in *Not-God* summarized, evolves from the "shared honesty of mutual vulnerability openly acknowledged."

When a patient arrived and was feeling well enough, Carroll or Zapp would talk to him privately in the meeting room (called the "Amen" corner) and conduct what today would formally be called the intake, the assessment, and the diagnostic. Zapp recalled sessions he would have with newly arrived patients.

> We would talk alone and I would find out about him and form my impressions. [In] those days you could tell who was going to stay sober and who wasn't by their attitude.

Is it any wonder, given the sometimes suffocating licensure and accreditation requirements, that the counselor yearns for the "good old days" when things were simpler?

Carroll seemed to be everywhere and presided with an almost messianic presence. In regard to Hazelden's program, he was influential in shaping the opinions and attitudes of both Zapp and Lon Jacobson, who succeeded Zapp as Carroll's assistant in 1958. Zapp and Jacobson concurred that Carroll was skillful in orchestrating the personalities of the men who worked for him, so there was a minimum of discord.

A medical component of treatment was present but primitive. Most of the men went cold turkey upon arrival. The routine was to let a man sleep off his alcohol. In severe cases, "blue and whites" (Amytal Sodium) or "yellow jackets" (Sodium Nembutal) were used. Dr. Harold Albrecht from Lindstrom, Minnesota would come out to administer IV's. "For the really tough cases he would administer a needle," Zapp said of Dr. Albrecht, "which he called his ace-in-the-hole."

When someone had delirium tremens, he was generally cared for at Hazelden. When things really got bad for a patient, he was taken to the nearby St. Croix Clinic in Wisconsin. According to Zapp:

> We drove one fellow down in the station wagon with windows wide open in the dead of winter because he was very hot; later we found out he had pneumonia. [The patient survived the ordeal.]

Convulsions were common. Staff and patients would sit on a man and put a clothespin in his mouth, which Zapp said

> worked as well as anything. And we prayed that he wouldn't die. One man convulsed a month after he arrived and broke all the teeth in his lower jaw.

Physical therapy took the form of multiple recreational activities: hiking, shuffleboard, table tennis, skiing, and tobogganing. The Butlers provided a pool table in 1950. There was some winter fishing on the adjacent lake. Carroll wrote: "The question of summer recreation is not as pressing a problem as a more extensive winter program." This was clear evidence that Hazelden's location was in Minnesota where the four seasons have been described as winter, June, July, and August.

Physiological therapy during and after withdrawal consisted of administering vitamin B shots, accompanied by yeast tablets. "The yeast tablets had the startling effect of causing black stools," Zapp said, "and the names given them were colorful."

Whenever anyone asked for something because he was feeling bad, Zapp, who did not believe in giving pills, would hand him a placebo. Everyone thought he was a pretty swell guy.

Some admission procedures were similar to the present process. Individuals could be received any time of the day and night. A patient's luggage was thoroughly checked upon arrival. But then, as now, patients were ingenious at inventing new ways of smuggling the proscribed onto the premises. Zapp recalled:

> One time . . . Chet [Burke] caught a plant that was sent to a patient by his wife, and all over it were glued little red pills. You couldn't see them unless you looked closely.

Early on Hazelden relied on the group conscience and peer pressure to prevent and discourage patients from smuggling alcohol and pills onto the grounds.

In the young days, pressure and restraints were at a minimum. Car keys were never collected. The men were allowed to go into Center City; a station wagon was available for that purpose. The patients who were still shaky were persuaded not to go. "Sometimes there were problems," Zapp reminisced, "like the time a fellow brought back a suspicious amount of hair tonic."

There was no established policy as to the length of stay. The general idea was to persuade the patients to remain as long as the counselor felt was necessary. The lecture cycle was completed in three weeks and served as the parameter for the standard treatment period, although many remained longer.

The greatest difficulty was in persuading patients to remain the first week. Once that chore was accomplished, it was easier to keep the patient for the three weeks. Zapp recalled:

> The worst time of the year was the income tax period. Men would come in just sober enough to panic at the thought of making out their tax returns and rush off home to take care of it. Of course, they would arrive home drunk and then have to be shipped right back to Hazelden.

From its inception Hazelden responded to the legitimate religious needs of its patients. Carroll insisted patients attend church, if only for the discipline it involved. Catholics attended Father Winzerling's parishes in Taylors Falls and Franconia, Minnesota for the Sunday Mass/Liturgy. Protestants attended the Lutheran church in Center City. Later on, Jewish patients would be transported to the Twin Cities at their request.

One of the unique aspects of Hazelden's treatment program was the emphasis placed on the Fifth Step: an alcoholic admitting to another person the exact nature of his wrongs. Hazelden encouraged, even pressured, patients to take the Fifth Step before leaving. Zapp was opposed to an alcoholic being involved in another alcoholic's Fifth Step; he felt the possibility of a breach of confidence was always present should the receiver lapse into drinking. According to Zapp:

> Father Winzerling was available to Catholic patients at Hazelden, but with the exception of the Lutheran minister at Center City who understood and accepted alcoholics, there was some difficulty encountered in involving Protestant

ministers in Fifth Step taking.

Patients then, as now, were made to feel at home. The A.A. program was presented, but the men who got well did it mostly on their own. Then, as now, they were the ones who began to internalize the Steps, however little or in depth initially.

Reflection: On the Validity of an Inpatient Program

By 1937 the cofounders of A.A., Bill W. and Dr. Bob, were convinced their experience of recovery was valid, and could and should be shared with other alcoholics. As one way of assisting the alcoholic, they considered the construction and operation of a chain of hospitals, specializing in the treatment of alcoholism.

Today the establishment of hospital-based rehabilitation programs has become a lucrative and expanding business. This was not always the case. When the A.A. movement began, most general hospitals were unwilling to offer any care to alcoholics. As Kurtz in *Not-God* wrote:

> Hospitals at that time were reluctant to admit alcoholics under *any* diagnosis, less over moral or treatment concerns, than because of the blunt fact that alcoholics rarely paid their bills.

The American Hospital Association's recognition of alcoholism as a disease in 1954 alleviated some of the hospitals' hesitation, but not totally. Insurance benefits for the disease removed most of any lingering reluctance.

Carroll recollected his own experience in 1940:

> They would not take an alcoholic into any hospital that I knew of at that time — I remember at one time that I was down to Mankato, and was doing quite a lot of drinking. I went up to a Catholic hospital and wanted to get in and they told me to sit down. Then the priest came down and told me to get the hell out of there or he'd call the police. That's what they used to think of the alcoholic.

There was every good reason for A.A.'s cofounders to consider the possibility of operating a chain of hospitals. Dr. Bob was leary about the idea of profit-making hospitals, and the concept was rejected outright by the Akron, Ohio A.A. group. At the same time, it was clear many alcoholics needed medical and hospital care as well as some time apart from a predisposing environment. Kurtz described how these two elements were combined in the development of the alcoholic unit at St. Thomas Hospital in Akron.

In the spring of 1939, Dr. Bob confessed his alcoholism to Sister Ignatia of the Sisters of Charity of St. Augustine, which staffed St. Thomas Hospital. Dr. Bob and Sister Ignatia conspired to smuggle or "bootleg" alcoholics into the hospital, the usual diagnosis being acute gastritis. Sister Ignatia's own scruples took her to the parish priest of St. Martin's, Father Vincent Haas. After listening to Sister Ignatia and attending an A.A. meeting of the Clevelanders in Akron, Father Haas viewed A.A. as a "movement just like the early Franciscans." His support and discernment accomplished two things. It encouraged Sister Ignatia to bring the matter to the administrator of St. Thomas, thereby formalizing and sanctioning the treatment of alcoholics in the hospital. It also allayed the fears of the staunch Catholics of the Cleveland group about the program of A.A.

Aside from the question of hospital treatment for the physical consequences of the disease, another equally important point has to be made. When alcoholics from Cleveland had been detoxified by Dr. Bob at the hospital, these men, according to Kurtz in *Not-God*,

> usually spent a few weeks in Akron — sharing the daily round of camaraderie that characterized these years. Eventually, however, they had to return to their families and — if lucky —their jobs in Cleveland.

This was the seminal idea of a supportive environment to assist alcoholics in thinking straight and indoctrinating them with the A.A. program. Because the A.A. community in the Twin Cities favored the notion of a supportive environment, this contributed to the idea, genesis, and success of the Hazelden experiment. At Hazelden, a triad of elements worked in concert: sober surroundings, the A.A. program, and a counselor who could translate the program through his own experience in a meaningful way for his guest.

Moreover, the medical (hospital) component was attached. From the moment Hazelden opened, a doctor was available; by 1954 a consulting contract had been worked out with St. Croix Clinic, and four physicians were consultants at Hazelden on a part-time basis.

In the early days when Hazelden was just a concept, a variety of terms were employed to describe it — a hospital, a sanatorium, a guest house, a country retreat, and more. All these terms sought to capture the nature of this new experiment. As a matter of record, Hazelden was described as a hospital in its charter of incorporation. While the innocuous name, Hazelden, says little, in its entirety Hazelden does respond to all elements of a preeminent treatment program as required by the Joint Commission on Accreditation of Hospitals. Nevertheless, from its very beginning Hazelden simply addressed a need many alcoholics had for a separate, supportive environment. And reciprocally, history and success have attested to the validity of that need.

*"Made a decision to turn
our will . . ."
from Step Three*

4. Enter the Butlers —
The Corporate Culture

PATIENTS WERE RECOVERING and leading productive lives.
Some stability had been provided with the departure of Ripley
and the incorporation of Hazelden under the direction of Lilly. But
while corporate structure was important, financial stability was
essential. This was the major issue throughout 1949-1951. While
the patient census continued to increase, it was often very low,
and revenues were never enough to cover operating costs. Kerwin and McGarvey had reassured Carroll they would be able to
raise an extra $15,000 a year for operating expenses, but that never
materialized.

Fund-raising efforts were very often frustrating and fatiguing. A
point arrived when Carroll, after a trip to the Twin Cities, was so
discouraged at not having obtained sufficient monies that he
stopped by the side of the road and prayed: "If it be God's will, it
[Hazelden] will prosper." He turned it over and never worried
about it again. Such was the nature of Lynn Carroll's program.

Carroll's program carried Hazelden through its early years until
the Butler family purchased the option from Lilly and provided
the moral support and financial stability to assure Hazelden's
permanency. The following events led to the crisis that involved
the withdrawal of Lilly's backing and the intervention of the
Butler family.

Chapter 2 has described how Lilly purchased the Power estate
through the Coyle Foundation, which resold it to Hazelden for
$50,000 to be paid in annual installments of $2,000 plus 4 percent
interest. Hazelden was unable to meet these payments. Furthermore, the cost of all the furniture, oriental rugs, and remaining
furnishings on the Power estate amounted to $11,500. Add to this

Patrick Butler — 1958

another four to five thousand dollars worth of equipment and furniture acquired during the remainder of 1949. These purchases necessitated borrowing another $15,000 in October 1949. Consequently, at the end of 1949, Hazelden had two outstanding notes totalling $65,000.

Only half the operating cost in 1949 was accounted for by patient revenue. When Carroll reported to the board in January 1950, he noted there were not more than four patients at Hazelden at any one time for approximately the previous three weeks. (It had been estimated that an average of seven to eight patients per day would cover the operating costs.) The question of finances was a major topic during the board meeting, and Lilly hoped the board would raise $100,000 during 1950.

To be on the safe side, McGarvey, the unofficial fund-raiser, set a target of raising $30,000. During the previous year, his efforts had yielded excellent results, raising $19,955 which included three big gifts of $5,000 each from Charles A. Ward, president and general manager of Brown and Bigelow; the I. A. O'Shaughnessy Foundation; and R. C. Lilly through the Coyle Foundation.

In order to assist in the fund-raising and in the census, a brochure was prepared under the direction of Ward, who was a personal friend of Lilly. Titled *Inspiration for Recovery*, the brochure contained a clear message about Hazelden's goals and objectives. It was sent with a cover letter by Lilly to over 2,500 people, including probate court judges, doctors in Minnesota, North Dakota and South Dakota, and companies and firms in the Twin Cities. This same brochure was sent to the A.A. squad leaders in the Twin Cities; it included a letter from Carroll explaining elements of the program and Hazelden's rates ($100 for the first week, and $85 per week thereafter), and asked the squad leaders to recommend Hazelden to any alcoholic they encountered who needed treatment.

Despite the brochure and McGarvey's efforts at fund-raising, the results were hardly encouraging. The big contribution was missing. Moreover, people sought to avoid McGarvey, who would ask his A.A. friends for an occasional $100. This support was neither substantial nor could it be counted on to continue. Patrick Butler recalled:

> I was talking to Norvy M., one of the old-timers in Minneapolis A.A., and he related that they would all try to duck Bob McGarvey because he had an arm out for us either to send us up to Hazelden or to hit us over the head for a hundred or so. But that type of support did not last very

long. . . . A.A. itself was struggling . . . and of course, the old saying in A.A. is that when alcoholics get sober they get tight. They begin paying their own debts.

By the end of 1950 McGarvey had raised only $1,800. The major contributors were Lawrence Butler, who was Patrick's brother, and Emmett Butler, who was the father of Lawrence and Patrick. Together, they gave $1,300 of the total. The total amount raised was a far cry from the $100,000 hoped for by Lilly, or the $30,000 hoped for by McGarvey. This lack of financial support would signal the departure of Lilly and the entrance of the Butler family in 1951.

When Hazelden had forfeited its payment for 1950 on the note to the Coyle Foundation, Lilly had thought of foreclosing but apparently Ward had talked him into giving Hazelden some more time. Lilly agreed and, as late as April 1951, he wrote to the Hill Foundation requesting a renewal of its financial support. He believed Hazelden was making progress, though slowly, in building support for its work. He anticipated that donations and the number of paying patients would increase in the next few years.

It came as a surprise two weeks later that Lilly decided to foreclose on the contract for deed on which Hazelden had defaulted. He called a special meeting of the Hazelden board on 7 May 1951. He reported that he had an offer from the Sisters of St. Joseph in Crookston, Minnesota to purchase the land, buildings, furnishings, and equipment at Hazelden for $60,000. Lilly stated that if Hazelden were to pay $45,000 within 30 days, the Coyle Foundation would pay off the $12,500 note covering the furniture and equipment. If Hazelden could not come up with the money, the Coyle Foundation would repossess the property and sell it to the Sisters of St. Joseph. This was a critical juncture in Hazelden's history.

It was difficult at that time to assess precisely Lilly's reasons for his decision. T. D. Maier, who was vice president and treasurer of the Coyle Foundation, believed the primary reason for the proposed sale was Lilly's disappointment that priests were not taking advantage of the facility. Of secondary importance, according to Maier, was Lilly's general dissatisfaction at Hazelden's inability to meet its payments to the Coyle Foundation.

At the same time, Lilly's offer to cover the note for the furniture and equipment at Hazelden was a generous one as he sought to disengage the Coyle Foundation from the project.

Carroll wrote to McGarvey: "The ultimatum laid down by Lilly has to be met if Hazelden is to be carried on."

It appears that the Butler family, particularly Patrick, was aware of Lilly's reluctance to continue his support. Butler recalled an unplanned conversation he had with Lilly early in 1951, either before or after a golf game at the Somerset Country Club in St. Paul. During the course of the conversation, Lilly suggested the Butlers take over Hazelden.

According to Butler, Lilly thought the nuns from the Sisters of St. Joseph could administer Hazelden in a fiscally responsible fashion, and then A.A. could direct the program.

The Butlers were gifted in business and finance through their involvement in the heavy construction and mining industries. Because they also were genuinely concerned about the world of the alcoholic, they realized Lilly was making an attractive proposal. Patrick Butler reminisced:

> It was partly our interest in Hazelden and partly the idea of getting a bargain from Lilly — he was a sharp cookie.

Carroll recalled the chain of events that led eventually to the Butler intervention:

Lilly could not be persuaded to change his mind about foreclosing. On 8 May 1951, the day after Lilly had announced his recall of the mortgage, Lawrence Butler, a member of Hazelden's board, encouraged by Patrick's golfing conversation with Lilly, took Carroll with him to see the "old man," Emmett Butler. Patrick Butler was also present that day in Emmett's office. Emmett Butler, who had stopped drinking in 1945, obviously had an interest in Hazelden because of its impact on his two sons.

While Carroll waited outside Emmett's office, the father and his two sons discussed the Hazelden situation and Lilly's offer. Finally, Lawrence Butler appeared and announced to Carroll: "Well, it's settled, we're taking over," signifying that Hazelden would continue with the Butlers assuming both financial responsibility and prominent positions on the board.

On 5 June 1951, the Coyle Foundation assigned the contract for deed to Emmett, Patrick, and Lawrence Butler.

While the important intervention of the Butlers in 1951-1952 was not inevitable, the initial linkage had already been forged by the family's strong desire to help the alcoholic and by the fact that the Butlers had already been involved with Hazelden in a variety of ways. Lawrence Butler was the first patient at Hazelden (21 April 1949), and was elected to the board of trustees shortly thereafter. Patrick Butler was a patient at Hazelden twice: once in 1949 and again in 1950. Carroll's 1949 report to the board of trustees singled out Lawrence Butler for his special and continued assistance to Hazelden. In 1950 the Butlers made generous contributions.

With the Butlers' involvement, Hazelden's viability was assured. Their dedication, loyalty, and compassion provided Hazelden with a sense of direction and a spirit of humanity and service, all of which were to evolve into the gracefully nurtured *caring community* concept.

The arrival of the Butlers eased the fiscal pressures on Carroll, who made Hazelden a household word in the Midwest during the fifties. At the beginning of October 1951, Carroll, who had earlier made a decision to turn the whole financial problem over to a Higher Power, was able to write to McGarvey that finances were fairly good and there was a possibility of breaking even by the end of the year, "which will indeed be remarkable after the short time we have been in operation." He was concerned, however, that there was still no reserve or operating capital to fall back on.

Carroll knew Hazelden's ultimate financial security rested with the Butlers. He knew Patrick Butler had been very busy and active, spending a great deal of time at the state hospital in Willmar, Minnesota. Butler also sought to form an advisory council for Hazelden. Carroll believed Butler would be raising a sizeable sum "so that we will have some cushion to fall back on." This did happen. The Butler family's financial commitment was formally secured by the end of 1952.

In December of that year the Hazelden Board of Trustees was reorganized; the members included Carroll, Heckman, Lilly, and Emmett, Lawrence, and Patrick Butler. Patrick Butler was chosen president. What evolved was an active and responsible family board. The Butler family would be prominently represented on the board in the decades to come.

At the time when the board was reorganized, a promissory note of $75,000 was deposited with the First National Bank of St. Paul, for two purposes:

1. Forty-five thousand dollars was to retire the purchase loan held by the bank.
2. The remaining $30,000 could be drawn on when necessary for the operation of Hazelden or for the expansion of its facilities.

The operating cushion Carroll had desired was now a reality.

Patrick Butler became more and more involved with the everyday affairs of Hazelden. He had retired at the age of 48 when the Butler brothers sold their Mesabi Range iron ore holdings. At that time, Butler was at loose ends and bored, and became virtually devoted to drinking. His recovery in 1950 and the Butler financing of Hazelden in 1951 provided him with a sense of purpose and filled a void in his life. His weekly trips to Center City, which started at that time, allowed him to become intimately and personally aware of the details of the program and its needs. The pilgrimage became an uninterrupted custom for 35 years. No corporate president was any more aware of complex events and people in the evolution of a company. Butler's intervention in the major and minor details of Hazelden was soon to become a cause of some friction between Carroll and himself.

At the end of 1952 Hazelden had moved from a very precarious situation to a secure and settled stage. At that time, Patrick Butler provided a summary report on Hazelden's three and one-half years of operation. Some four hundred men had been "guests" at Hazelden. Butler reported that 56 percent had returned "to normal living without liquor; 25 percent have made good progress, and have an excellent chance of ultimate recovery; 10 percent have shown slight progress but may, eventually, make the grade; the balance have indicated no progress or are no longer living."

In the first year of Hazelden's operation, 1949, the average number of patient days (that is, the average number of patients at Hazelden per day) was 4.4, which increased to 7.3 in 1952. Costs had risen so that while the estimated break-even point was eight patient days in 1949, it was ten in 1952. The estimated operating deficit for 1952 was $15,000.

Capital expenditures for 1952 came to $25,000 — including a new wing with eight rooms; an office; a reception room; a car for the manager, Carroll; a station wagon for transportation; and the conversion from coal to oil heat.

Butler's summary ended with what continued to be his own and Hazelden's hallmark: "The property has been maintained in excellent condition."

The Butler family provided structure, stability, support, and above all, concern for the dignity of each individual alcoholic. Butler described over 30 years ago what today would be called "the corporate culture" and character:

> The satisfaction, I think, that we should feel is that we are helping more and more men each year. We believe that the new facilities are going to make the place more attractive;

Patrick and Aimee Mott Butler break ground for 1964 expansion project

certainly we shall be able to do a better job for the comfort of our clients.

The Butler family, particularly Patrick and Aimee Mott Butler, who married in 1926, occupy the preeminent place in the history of Hazelden. In many respects Hazelden became a family affair in the sense that Aimee and Patrick adopted Hazelden as their family.

Patrick Butler had an instinct for the concept (continuum of care); an instinct for detail; an instinct for the pragmatic (fill beds, balance the budget); and an instinct for the beauty of the environment through responding to the need for the alcoholic's dignity.

For over three decades Aimee and Patrick Butler were (and continue as) creative and respected leaders in the field of chemical dependency, providing the opportunity and environment for thousands of men and women of all ages to reclaim, rehabilitate, and reconstruct their lives.

*"Made direct amends to
such people wherever
possible, except when to
do so would injure them
or others."*
Step Nine

5. Fellowship Club

MINNESOTA'S CONTINUUM OF CARE for chemical dependency was not the result of a master design carefully put in place component by component by inspired planners. This continuum of care was developed over the course of many years and ranged from prevention to intervention, including a wide variety of services covering, among others, inpatient and outpatient treatment.

The differing needs of chemically dependent people evoked different levels of care. All of the following situations contributed to the development of Minnesota's continuum of care:

- the degree and the type of the problem;
- the problem's longevity;
- the number of associated problems;
- the amount of external support (family and friends);
- the person's motivation to change;
- the person's ability to deal with issues in treatment.

Fellowship Club (the name was provided by Patrick Butler) was a response to a pressing human need. It was established in 1953 for men who were homeless and needed time to adjust to economic and social realities without using alcohol for support. It wasn't until 1979 that women were admitted, when a new wing was completed that allowed them to be integrated into the program, previously restricted to males. The concept of a halfway house and, in this case, Fellowship Club, was fostered by Patrick Butler's experiences in the early fifties at Willmar State Hospital where he spent a great deal of time and was in constant contact with Nelson Bradley, who was the driving force behind rehabilitating alcoholics at the hospital.

Alcoholics who were treated at Willmar State Hospital would return to their home communities without a job, a place to stay, or

Fellowship Club

money for the simple necessities of life. Because of their location, they were often unable to have good linkage with the A.A. fellowship. It was clear that some kind of residential aftercare was needed. Hence, the beginning of the halfway house concept.

The story is that in 1953 Patrick Butler and Hazelden board member George Nienaber and their mutual friend Father Curtin were discussing the plight of an alcoholic whom the three of them knew. Despite repeated treatments, the alcoholic was unable to maintain sobriety. What was needed, the three of them decided, was a "halfway house," so that the alcoholic could gradually gather strength and regain a role in society.

At about the same time, the Archdiocese of St. Paul was trying to interest the Butler family in purchasing a large, vacant home at 341 North Dale Street, St. Paul. Thus, the genesis of Fellowship Club was the result of a number of factors converging at the right time and the right place.

The large home on North Dale Street was converted to a halfway house for alcoholics in December 1953. It had been previously maintained as a Catholic infants' home by the Sisters of St. Joseph. The property was purchased from the Archdiocese of St. Paul by Hazelden for $20,000, and Hazelden authorized a further $5,000 to renovate the building for a fifteen bed halfway house.

Fellowship Club ran into a great deal of opposition from those who considered it detrimental to the neighborhood. Shortly after Fellowship Club's opening, residents of the area strongly objected to having a "rest home" for alcoholics in their neighborhood.

A petition for Fellowship Club's licensure was rejected by the St. Paul City Council. In 1954, the *Minneapolis Spokesman* reported that, during the hearings, a civic leader who represented the area residents opposed to Fellowship Club's licensure "stressed the fact that the community, already burdened with many problems of its own, should not be made to take on another [problem], especially since most of its residents are bound to this area through prejudice."

The *Minneapolis Spokesman* further related:

> Each of the speakers [at the hearings] were graphic in their description of the harm already done to the community, producing witnesses who had experienced frightening experiences as a result of activities of residents of the home [Fellowship Club].

When the Hazelden Foundation refused to close Fellowship Club, the city council brought the matter to court. After being litigated for about a year, the court proceedings were recessed indefinitely in October 1955. Fellowship Club never ceased to operate during this period.

Fellowship Club was open to any man who was homeless, penniless, and friendless because of alcoholism. It was established to provide three corresponding ingredients for recovery: a home, a job, and friends who had the same problems. The Fellowship Club guest became a member of a group and soon came to realize that others with problems as great or greater than his managed to do something about them.

In order to reestablish an individual sense of responsibility, each Fellowship Club guest was expected to find a job and, shortly thereafter, he would be charged for room and board — $21 per week. The North Dale Street home had sleeping rooms for staff and residents, a complete kitchen, dining facilities, and recreation and reading rooms.

The conditions for acceptance were few and simple. The individual had to be single (which extended to being divorced or separated), and his background had to demonstrate a problem with alcohol. Another obviously important condition for admission was that the alcoholic had to be "dry," not having had any liquor for at least twelve hours. Staff screening was thorough. It was difficult to "con" staff since every member of the original staff was a recovering alcoholic.

The new guest was first assigned a bed in a large room. If he demonstrated he was eager and willing to stop drinking, he could move into a four- or two-man room. If he stayed long enough, his seniority would grant him a single room.

After a brief indoctrination period in A.A. philosophy and Fellowship Club's operation and rules, the guest was provided a job away from Fellowship Club — as a day laborer cutting grass or putting up screens, or as a janitor, mechanic, or painter. Three nights per week there was an A.A. meeting at Fellowship Club and all guests were expected to attend. The number one rule at Fellowship Club was, no liquor. A guest would be immediately expelled for a violation. He could reapply after 60 days. But after three repeats, he was permanently expelled.

Fellowship Club was a home. An atmosphere of intimacy was provided by caring people. Reminiscing on "the good old days," the *Fellowship Club Newsletter* recalled how John Cook, the director of Fellowship Club from 1953 to 1956, "would always be waiting to greet us when we returned home from work at the end of the day and offer encouragement and a pat-on-the-back, and, once in awhile, a verbal kick in the pants when we needed it."

Frank Kaiser, well known for his work with alcoholics and previously the secretary of "2218" in Minneapolis, was Fellowship Club's employment counselor until 1955. Kaiser and Cook provided a straight from the shoulder A.A. program.

Pat Butler visited often and helped the men realize just what is meant by the expression "but for the Grace of God" and the spiritual aspect of the program. He also provided lectures on golfing and smoking, remarking that Walter Hagen, the famous golfer, never chain-smoked.

Speakers from other A.A. groups and squads conducted the Friday night discussion classes. The serious was always spiked with humor, such as this anecdote from the newsletter:

> Ole O. gave an inspiring talk. He mixed a little humor in with his comments and evoked quite a roar from the men when he related how on one of his binges he had purchased a cow and then completely forgot about it until a few days later when a live kicking cow was delivered to his door. This might have been all right had not Ole and his wife been living in a modest three-room apartment in the heart of the city.

Camaraderie, casualness, and liquorless conviviality always remained a hallmark of Fellowship Club. People were encouraged to drop in anytime for a cup of coffee. About 150 friends and alumni celebrated Fellowship Club's third anniversary in 1956. Nelson Bradley was the featured lecturer and spoke on "Alcohol as an Anesthetic." The *Hazelden Newsletter* reported "all the guests were furnished a good snack (for free, yet)."

The following quote from the *Fellowship Club Newsletter* exemplifies the sense of community and family that prevailed at Fellowship Club.

> Since Fellowship Club opened up we've had a dog (named John), a cat (named Muscatel), and now this (a parakeet)! Is this surprising? — The bird book says that parakeets can more easily master words beginning with the letters P.B. Fitz says it should stand for "Pretty Bird," but I wonder.

This was a faintly disguised reference to Patrick Butler.

As at Hazelden, Fellowship Club's approach was simple, providing its guests with a clean place to rest and sleep, good and abundant food, lectures, and the opportunity to share with other alcoholics and to internalize the A.A. principles. The program was

The early Fellowship Club on Dale Street

also directed at the reactivation of the individual's work and social life, without alcohol. An added dimension was the occupational therapy class in leather and copper tooling.

Staff came and went rapidly. In February 1956, John Cook resigned as director and was replaced by Bud MacCallister Gordon.

Flowers and plants graced the home; floral displays greeted the guests and visitors at the front entrance. The summer house in the backyard, which had been considered an eyesore, suddenly took on a new appearance when the men cleaned and painted it; they also sanded and painted the lawn and porch furniture. And a martin birdhouse was erected.

For the interior, Aimee Butler supplied a new sofa, rugs, and lamps to brighten up the living room. The men appreciated what was being done. The newsletter observed, "We notice, too, how much more use [the living room] is getting now."

As at Hazelden, so at Fellowship Club, everything was done to remove whatever could be dehumanizing and install whatever might enhance individual and group dignity.

During the summer of 1957, preliminaries to condemnation proceedings were started on Fellowship Club by the Minnesota Department of Highways in order to build the Interstate 94 expressway. This necessitated the search for a new residence which was found at 680 Stewart Avenue, St. Paul. The new Fellowship Club, an old mansion, as former St. Paul newspaper columnist Oliver Towne wrote, "with its rows of stain glass windows, Edwardian fireplaces, ornately carved dark woods and bannisters of the dark staircase," was built in the 1880s from the beer profits by the Bannholzer Van Hoven family. The home stands in clear view of the Schmidt Brewery sign on West Seventh Street in St. Paul.

Many had expressed both joy and sorrow about leaving the 341 North Dale Street home, but, according to the newsletter, the guests could "hardly wait to settle down [in the new residence] by the fireplace in its spacious living room, and browse around in the basement recreation room and loaf a bit in the two downstairs lounges. Even our long hoped for gymnasium may become a reality when the old schoolroom can be converted."

There were other sentiments as well. When "341" was to be torn down, the newsletter observed, "The old place looks better and better every day. There will always be a '341 Fellowship Club' in the hearts and minds of each and every one of the men who have shared in its fellowship."

The move to the new facility occurred in October 1958 and was celebrated by having not one, but two open houses. Despite the adverse conditions surrounding Fellowship Club's inception, the North Dale Street Fellowship Club had been a success; both the staff and guests could look back over the first five years with pride.

Fellowship Club had always been a steady performer. At the beginning of 1958, its population was between 25 and 30 residents, and the length of stay had increased from about 40 days to a little over 60.

This same spirit and success spilled over to the Stewart Avenue Fellowship Club. A humanizing spirit unfolded: the yard took shape after hours of effort from all the men. Flower beds were put in, bushes were planted in front of the porches, and the fence was painted, all adding up to a magnificent park-like setting.

The new Fellowship Club was productive from the first year of operation. In 1959, a total of 107 men had been through Fellowship Club. The average age kept getting lower — 37.8 years old, or four years under the 1958 average.

Eighty-six of the 107 men were placed in regular full-time jobs. According to the newsletter, thanks were due to

> the chairmen of the boards, down through the personnel offices to the men at the next machine or the next desk, who through their sympathetic understanding have exhibited their faith, their charity, and their trust in Fellowship Club by helping us climb this stairway of the second chance through employment.

And with the help of the clergy, 25 men were reunited with their families.

Such success breeds expansion, which was planned and completed in 1960. Living quarters increased from 30 to 40 resident beds. A new dining room, dishwashing area, and kitchen were completed. And a new library and coffee room were added in 1961, the same year that Dr. Daniel Anderson was hired as executive vice president of Hazelden and established his office and home base at the newly-renovated Fellowship Club.

By 1963, when Fellowship Club had completed a decade of service, its bed capacity had increased to 41. During those ten years, Fellowship Club was able to rehabilitate hundreds of desocialized alcoholics and restore them as productive members of their communities by providing room and board, indoctrination into the philosophy of A.A., individual and group therapy, and counseling on unemployment, social problems, and job placement. These were alcoholics who had no family ties, no stable job history, or were completely dependent upon public support. It often developed that the majority of men accepted at Fellowship Club were on probation or parole or were recently discharged from local jails or state alcoholism facilities. Some had been discharged from veterans' hospitals while others were classified as local or national transients.

Fellowship Club gradually established cooperative relationships with the Minnesota Division of Vocational Rehabilitation and with institutions functioning under the Minnesota Department of Public Welfare, such as Willmar State Hospital, and Moose Lake State Hospital in Moose Lake, Minnesota. Moreover, Hazelden gradually began to send its clients to Fellowship Club for aftercare, so that the idea of a halfway house began to emerge as a component of the rehabilitative continuum of care as it is understood today.

Aimee and Patrick Butler with Orv Larson

Perhaps Orv Larson has had the most important impact on Fellowship Club. In November 1961 when he completed treatment in North Dakota, Larson feared leaving because he had no place to go nor anyone to lend him support in his recovery from alcoholism. He learned of Fellowship Club from the director of the treatment program in North Dakota. The director told him of a halfway house in Minnesota where recovering alcoholics could find work and receive support from people in similar situations.

Arriving at Fellowship Club unannounced at the end of 1961, Larson was given a cot next to the pool table. One week later, he met Patrick Butler, who repeated his name: "Larson, Larson, sounds Scandinavian." Larson replied affirmatively with pride. Butler then asked Larson how it was that he came by the Irish disease. This initial exchange was the beginning of a lifelong friendship.

Butler perceived in Larson a great strength. He asked him in 1962 to stay on as assistant to the director. The following year Larson became director, a position he still holds in 1987.

Larson's personal job experiences taught him a job's therapeutic value for the recovering alcoholic. In 1962 he received $1.50 per hour for a painting job while others who were still drinking on the job received $2.50 per hour. The reason he was paid less, he discovered, was that he admitted his problem of alcoholism although he no longer drank, and the public stigma saw him as less valuable than the on-the-job drinker.

During his time at Fellowship Club, Larson was able to establish a network of job referrals second to none in the Twin Cities. His is one of the principal reasons that Fellowship Club maintains a national position as a premier halfway house for chemically dependent men and women.

Despite many attractive offers to change jobs, Larson has stayed at Fellowship Club for more than twenty years as a tireless, caring, and compassionate leader. His greatest strength, of course, comes from his own homeless and alcoholic experience and his empathy for the guests who, because of their transient passage through Fellowship Club, have become stable sojourners in their journey through life. In preparation for that journey, Larson and Fellowship Club mapped out simple goals:

- social — the restoration of one's identity;
- vocational — the restoration of one's self-esteem;
- spiritual — the development of one's confidence (trust);
- re-creational — the rebirth of one's life-coping mechanisms.

The word "fellowship" has captured the significance of what a spiritual journey is all about: any spiritual journey through life is a community affair. Someone has to say, "I am with you."

"Look to this day, for it is Life, the life of all life. . . ."
Sanskrit proverb

6. The Willmar Connection

"THE ENTHUSIASM WE HAD at Willmar was really something — besides the energy — everyone was caught up in this — we ate and slept it. We talked about it in the coffee shop — we never let go of it. Now it's like another field. People come into it, and of course they are interested, but as you say — they learn about four times more slowly."

Thus did Nelson Bradley remember the early days at Willmar State Hospital where he was appointed superintendent in 1950.

It is not an easy task to capture in writing the early days at Willmar State Hospital. This was the beginning of the alcoholism treatment revolution of the fifties. The energy level at the hospital was extremely high; enthusiasm abounded; the people involved were caring, innovative, open, bright, and in many ways, prophetic. They did not resemble a scientific group of researchers, but a deeply-knit community, bound together by care and compassion for a population traditionally treated as parasites or pariahs.

It was an exciting period full of exhilarating events, creative ideas, and wonderful relationships. It was challenging. The staff was in crisis a great deal of the time, and they led a scrambling sort of existence. The people involved were never quite sure of what they were doing or where they were going. Many essential parts of the Minnesota Model developed quite by accident. The planning strategy was situational — scurrying from one task or meeting to the next. But marvelous things were accomplished. And those days will never return.

Willmar State Hospital, established in 1912, nestles in the rural community of Willmar in southwestern Minnesota about 100 miles west of Minneapolis. By its original charter, one of the hospi-

Nelson Bradley — inspiration for the Minnesota Model

tal's specific goals was the care and treatment of chronic alcoholics. As a result, Willmar State Hospital was the first of the seven state hospitals in Minnesota to serve as an "inebriate asylum" — the unenviable reference of that time to a treatment center for alcoholism.

Although the hospital was admitting alcoholics for years previous to 1950, there was no established program for alcoholics and no interest in developing one. Moreover, since it was also designated as a state hospital for mental patients, it reinforced the identification of alcoholism as a mental or psychiatric problem. Before the fifties, care at the hospital had been simply a question of "holding" patients — not an issue of treatment. This approach closely matched a similar attitude throughout the United States. The prevailing mood after the repeal of Prohibition in 1932 was one of skepticism and pessimism toward alcoholics — skepticism about alcoholics doing anything for themselves, and pessimism about doing anything for them.

The general public still viewed alcoholics as drunkards and moral reprobates. "It's their own fault for not being temperate," was a common judgment. Another line of thought was that drinking meant more to alcoholics than anything else in spite of the accidents and suicides that befell them. An added dimension of this attitude was that the social stigma surrounding alcoholics also surrounded people who associated with them. Thus people who somehow presumed that alcoholics were worthy of assistance or were entitled to being treated with some kindness or consideration were also held in contempt. As Daniel Anderson, who worked with Bradley at Willmar State Hospital, remarked, the prevailing attitude toward those who wanted to help alcoholics was the age-old condemnation by association or, sociologically, "derived stigma."

A major departure did occur, however, from the attitude concerning the unworthiness of alcoholics and their suitability for only the "snake pits" portrayed at that time. A more humane and caring approach within mental hospitals began in Minnesota and soon became a national movement.

In 1947, Dr. Nelson Bradley, a young medical student, was driving from Saskatchewan, Canada to a hospital in Michigan for his last year of surgical residency. His car broke down in the Twin Cities. That incident and a shortage of funds were sufficient reasons to finish his studies in Minnesota. He took a position as staff physician at Hastings State Hospital in Hastings, Minnesota, south of St. Paul, where he struck an enduring friendship with a young college student by the name of Daniel Anderson, who was working nights as an attendant. Both men were greatly influenced by the ideas of Dr. Ralph Rossen, superintendent of Hastings State Hospital. Rossen, who was soon to become the Commissioner of Mental Health in Minnesota, was guided by a simple theme, namely "to focus on each single day in the life of a patient, always trying to improve the quality of that life."

Rossen was influenced in his ideas by his administrative assistant, Fred Eiden. Rossen described Eiden as one of the three brightest people he had ever met. Eiden was to have a great impact on both Bradley and Anderson, as well as subsequent staff at Willmar regarding alcoholism and A.A. In fact, he could be described as their tutor and mentor in the evolution of the Minnesota Model.

When Bradley became superintendent at Willmar State Hospital in 1950, he persuaded Anderson to go with him as a recreation director (in reality, the low man on the totem pole). Anderson agreed, but asked Bradley, "What are we going to do?"

Bradley replied, "It's a 1,600 bed hospital, still a snake pit, but I think we can fix it up. They also have 30 to 40 'inebs' [inebriates] there." He asked Anderson if he knew anything about "inebs."

As expected of a young college student, Anderson replied: "No, we'll look it up though, and see what it is."

In the next few years the two men — Anderson the psychologist, and Bradley the psychiatrist — formed definite and progressive ideas about the treatment of alcoholics. Bradley was successful in implementing a radical departure from the psychiatric tradition in the conventional understanding of alcoholism.

Bradley made his first radical move in 1950. Shortly after his arrival at Willmar State Hospital in June, he initiated an open-door policy for the alcoholics who were angry about being locked-up. The results were remarkable. Before the open-door policy, about 22 percent of the hospital's alcoholics were running away. When the doors were unlocked, that number dropped to 6 percent. It was an audacious and risky, but successful step. Bradley intuitively recognized the need to separate the alcoholic from the stigma of mental illness, with its corollary of locked wards.

In the fall of 1950, a lecture series was started at the hospital by Bradley, who sought to orient the patients on the "44 Steps," which were the items identifying the various stages of alcoholism in the Jellinek Chart, named after Dr. E. M. Jellinek.

In 1951, the hospital's *Handbook on the Treatment of Alcoholism* described the elements of treatment.

1. Provision of as much psychiatric training as possible.
2. Presentation of the A.A. program.

By present standards, this would have been a great study in contrasts. But at that time it was the seed of the multidisciplinary team, which resulted in professionals from a variety of disciplines working with A.A. counselors.

Both Bradley and Anderson suspected that A.A. could provide the answer to the "inebs'" recovery. Although the two men did not understand A.A. very well, neither its philosophy nor its comic relief and jokes, they intuitively recognized that A.A.'s sense of humor was interwoven with deep spiritual insights.

A.A.'s success could not be identified in quantifiable terms because, as a voluntary association, it appeared to touch only a few alcoholics. Regarded by science as too simplistic and by organized religions as suspect because it was thought to be competitive with religion, A.A. appeared narrow in scope and limited in dogmatics. Finally, A.A. was also rejected by those alcoholics still suffering from the denial of their disease.

Why then were Bradley, Anderson, and Jean Rossi, a psychologist on staff at Willmar State Hospital, attracted to A.A.? They saw that A.A. could sober up alcoholics, and sustain them in their recovery. In A.A., alcoholics were willing to tell their "story," describing their past and present conditions to other alcoholics. Moreover, their continued sobriety, as well as their survival as practiced in the Twelfth Step, motivated them to work with alcoholics who were still drinking. Prior to 1950, professionals had little or no success in dealing with the inebriates. They simply did not know what to do with them. It was apparent to Bradley's team of professionals that A.A. people had phenomenal insights into the thinking and personalities of alcoholics. Although the inner workings of A.A. might have been a mystery to the Bradley team, it was evident that this self-help group worked — A.A. was successful in keeping some alcoholics sober.

Part of the A.A. tradition was its oral, didactic program. The development of the Minneapolis fellowship, for example, was a model of the origin and development of an A.A. group. Fred Eiden related:

> The Minneapolis [A.A.] group for all practical purposes was Pat Cronin in the beginning. The group rented a room or two in the vicinity of First Avenue South and Franklin. Later in 1942, they bought the house at 2218 1st Avenue South. As A.A. grew, the group itself was divided into smaller units

called squads. In the early days, and it was taken for granted that potential A.A. members were not people who read books, it became policy that when a new man was brought in, he was taken to Pat [Cronin] with the request that he explain A.A. to the new man. From this evolved "discussion groups" or "classes." I remember Pat giving the Twelve Steps in one "discussion" or "class"; later these twelve were divided into four discussions or classes. Some guy in Washington, D.C., produced a mimeographed pamphlet on the Twelve Steps and divided them as follows (which became the pattern in the Midwest); First Class: Step 1; Second Class: Inventory and Restitution: Steps 4, 5, 8, 9, and 10; Third Class: Spiritual: Steps 2, 3, 6, 7, and 11; and Fourth Class: Step 12.

The tradition handed on to novices, besides the written word (the Big Book), was the recovering alcoholic's personal understanding and experience of the Steps, program, and process of A.A. taught through older members' personal stories and examples. This process was to be translated into the treatment program at Willmar State Hospital.

During the early fifties, Bradley energetically cultivated the A.A. community in Willmar, the Twin Cities, and throughout Minnesota. Both Hazelden and Pioneer House were already treating alcoholics. In 1951, Bradley urged Glen Steele, a retired businessman and recovering alcoholic, to organize Saturday night A.A. meetings at Willmar State Hospital. Bradley recruited speakers from A.A. groups statewide — Otto Zapp from St. Cloud; Pat Cronin from "2218" in Minneapolis; Lynn Carroll from Hazelden; Fred Eiden from Hastings State Hospital; Patrick Butler from St. Paul; and Mel Brandes from the Midway A.A. group in St. Paul which was particularly supportive of the Willmar experiment. Bradley not only asked these men to speak, he asked them to advise him.

During the fall of 1951, on Bradley's initiative, Willmar State Hospital commenced a series of annual workshops to bring together professionals (doctors, nurses, clergy, and social workers) and A.A. people. By 1952, A.A. people were being encouraged to come to the hospital when the workday was ended to give lectures and visit with the patients.

Bradley knew what he had to do next: hire recovering alcoholics to assist with treatment. He had already, in 1952, surreptitiously hired Brandes of the Midway A.A. group as one of the hospital's employed Patient Agents. In 1953, the Bradley team approached the Minnesota Civil Service Commission with a request to hire recovering alcoholics as treatment counselors. They were met with skepticism and resistance. Finally, in 1954, John Jackson, the head of the Minnesota Civil Service Commission, created the state position of Counselor on Alcoholism, thanks to the Bradley team's persistence and the goodwill of Governor Elmer Anderson.

Bradley immediately went about gathering a pool of experienced recovering A.A. people. In 1954, Lowell Maxwell was the first Counselor on Alcoholism to be hired, with Fred Eiden following soon after. The hiring of these men assured that the A.A. program would soon permeate the entire treatment process. The patients were more open, spontaneous, and honest with counselors who were recovering alcoholics than they were with professionally trained behavior psychologists.

Another treatment strategy that gradually emerged at Willmar State Hospital was the peer group — patients helped each other by simply meeting informally in small, leaderless groups. The Counselors on Alcoholism were translating the function of A.A. meetings and the meaning of "one alcoholic talking to another over a cup of coffee" into treatment strategies in highly structured environments. The mutual assistance and support of other patients facing similar problems could be utilized beneficially by any group member. Dialogue was central and crucial to the process.

These new alcoholism counselors lectured on the symptoms of alcoholism, various characteristics of alcoholic behavior, the Twelve Steps, and techniques of positive change. This gradually evolved into a formal lecture series on a variety of topics related to alcoholism and change. The importance of the lecture became evident when it was moved from 4:30 P.M. to prime time at 8:30 A.M.

Willmar State Hospital already had its physicians, nurses, psychiatrists, psychologists, social workers, and recreation directors. Now, in 1954, the hospital had nondegreed Counselors on Alcoholism who were lay people — recovering alcoholics — sharing responsibility for a treatment program and having an equal say with psychiatrists, psychologists, and physicians. It is difficult today to imagine how radical a change this was, to go from a physician-oriented, psychoanalytic hospital to a treatment program conducted by "drunks."

This was a first and a remarkable revolution in the history of the

Daniel J. Anderson (left)
Mel Brandes and Nelson Bradley at Willmar (right)

human services delivery system. Of course, it did not happen all at once. The concept was revolutionary, but the process toward a multidisciplinary team was a gradual evolution and not without obstacles and resistance.

The working relationship between the recovering counselor and the psychologist was a case in point. Shortly after Fred Eiden was hired as a Counselor on Alcoholism, Anderson recalled:

> I can remember within the first year of Fred's arrival, while working with alcoholics who had terrible psychological problems. After shrinking their heads, I watched them get well right in front of me. They would thank me. Shake my hand, and say that they were going home — only to wind up back at Willmar again. This same patient would apologize to me saying that I had really helped him so much the last time. He really appreciated that and did feel better, but nonetheless he was still drinking. He would then add, "This time I think I'd better see what is going on in the A.A. program."

Anderson further recalled that he would read the "tea leaves" of a patient (a patient's Minnesota Multiphasic Personality Inventory) and see schizophrenia and perhaps an "assortment of other craziness." According to Anderson, he would tell Eiden:

> "Fred — this one's a real sick one." Eiden would say something stupid like: "I don't know, Dan, he seems to be getting

75

the program." That initially did not mean a thing to me because when one is that crazy — what did it mean "to get the program"? And who would win? Fred would win if this crazy guy stayed sober. And then on another occasion I would see a guy who was well. I tested him and said to Fred: "Fred, he's in good shape — not crazy — intelligent and should be a great surgeon someday (or something like that)." And Fred would say: "He doesn't have the program, though, Dan."

Eiden was to become a guide for a number of professionals who, besides Anderson, worked with alcoholics. Anderson and others were to learn that alcoholism was responsible for a great deal of "the craziness" — the irresponsible and self-defeating behavior in which the alcoholic engaged.

Though told with a sense of humor and humility, Anderson's story reveals the heart of the matter. The developing Minnesota Model would always maintain focus on the primary disease of alcoholism which needed a primary response: the A.A. program.

Although two necessary ingredients were present at Willmar State Hospital for a successful treatment program — the alcoholic patient who needed care, and a caring staff — the real problem was getting the team to work together. "Once we did get them working together, though," Anderson said, "it was almost miraculous."

The Reverend John Keller, who was sent by the Lutheran church to train at the hospital in alcoholism, recollected:

> I'd sit in a staff meeting at Willmar and see a recovering alcoholic disagree with a physician, but then they'd walk out and still be friends. It did not break their relationship. People were here to be together and bring their individual and collective knowledge and experience to provide the care the patients needed.

Gradually, things began to come together. The superfluous perquisites of professionalism were dropped almost naturally. The professionals surrendered their professional roles for the common team professionalism of assisting the alcoholic client. The team found itself sharing patients. The jealousy and turf associated with "my patient" was abandoned in the common dispensation of care.

Jean Rossi recalled that everyone was willing to give up their professional elitism in a common cause. They could not take their professionalism (which was not the same as their professional knowledge) too seriously. As the group personality developed, it maintained a principal ingredient: survival depended upon a sense of humor.

The mystery of the addictive need finally got through to the professionals. It was still a mystery, but its presence was recognized. The patients did indeed respond well. One of the patients in those early years recalled that the key ingredient was the acceptance of the alcoholic provided by all the staff. This mood spread throughout the hospital. This same patient recalled:

> I cannot say enough about the role models [the recovering counselors. They] looked professional, because they were professional. Moreover, they did not hide the fact that at times they disagreed with the physicians. Patients knew this went on. The frankness of staff promoted a high degree of trust. They were what you saw.

Dan Crowe, one of the early social workers on the Bradley team, described the education of both staff and patients as a "total immersion process." Crowe's own total immersion process included learning about alcoholism through on-unit experience and through the recovering alcoholic counselors. His own book knowledge counted for little or nothing in those days.

The total immersion process applied to the patients as well. There were daily lectures, daily A.A. meetings, group therapy, and even psychodrama. Various forms of recreation were also available. (Usually, however, a typical patient day was so filled with other activities that little time or energy was left for recreational pursuits.) There also was work therapy for the alcoholics — meaningful work which provided the opportunity, the first in a long time, to accomplish something.

The group camaraderie was a unique experience. According to Anderson:

> Everybody called everybody else, patients and staff alike, by their first names; drinking experiences and alcoholic histories were dramatically revealed at the slightest provocation; advice was freely given based on one's own experiential background of alcoholism and recovery; hope and enthusiasm were openly expressed about the good prospects that most patients had for recovery; and coffee was consumed extensively throughout the day and night.

But what would happen to the alcoholic outside the structured setting of Willmar State Hospital? The good prospects and hope for recovery needed another component. Bradley gave serious thought to this. The reality was that a person's recovery began the day upon leaving treatment. The importance of aftercare became evident.

As early as 1956, Bradley appointed Anderson to be director of the Willmar Alcoholic Follow Up Clinic at Willmar State Hospital. Two social workers, Lucille Poor and Bill McGee, were assigned to serve as aftercare counselors in the Twin Cities. This resulted in another piece of the continuum of care which became a combination aftercare and outpatient program to assist in the long-term recovery process after treatment. Efforts were thus begun to involve the total community in the program of alcoholism, and to involve patients in postinstitutional programs. Of course, A.A. was always there as the foundation. In isolated areas alcoholics and their families would be picked up and accompanied by other recovering alcoholics to aftercare centers or A.A. meetings 100 or 200 miles away.

Another startling addition to the multidisciplinary team at Willmar State Hospital was the clergy. At first, the growing Bradley team did not know what to do with the clergy. When the Reverend John Kauffmann was appointed the first full-time chaplain at the hospital, he was assigned as an assistant in the recreational program. But that was not for long. The Bradley team recognized that the clergy had a certain stability and could easily be trained to help alcoholics with their self-inventories (Step Four), and admission to another person of their character defects and inappropriate behavior (Step Five) — as the clergy at both Hazelden and Pioneer House were already doing.

Bradley always smiled when he recalled one of his earliest experiences with a clergyman-in-training.

> He was a very devout priest who would walk out of the room when the alcoholics were recounting their stories: "I slept with this woman or I did this." He finally left because he was unable to handle and listen to this type of public sharing.

Today there are all kinds of clergy people trained in alcoholism, but in the fifties most clergy people were ignorant about the disease. There were early exceptions like Father Clement Allard, who assisted alcoholics in taking the Fifth Step at Pioneer House; Father Oscar Winzerling, who did the same at Hazelden; and the Reverend Forrest Richeson whose church in Minneapolis attracted a large number of A.A. people whom he had assisted.

Willmar State Hospital — early forties

In 1952 the hospital began to sponsor a program of clinical training for future chaplains and resident pastors; this was a six-week-long summer training course with special emphasis on alcoholism. Furthermore, the Bradley team arranged one-day seminars in different parts of the state to familiarize clergy people of all faiths with the problem of alcoholism. These seminars would gradually make a significant impact by supporting the A.A. movement and fellowship.

Like the Reverend John Keller before him, the Reverend Gordon Grimm was sent by the Lutheran church in 1960 to train at Willmar State Hospital in alcoholism. Along with Keller, Grimm subsequently became an outstanding leader in the field of alcoholism. He became director of Hazelden's Training and Health Promotion Division. Keller eventually accompanied Bradley to Lutheran General Hospital in Chicago, where both continued to make outstanding contributions to the field of alcoholism treatment.

The presence of the clergy became an essential part of the multidisciplinary team because the clergy gave added and visible validation to the spiritual dimension of the A.A. program. Anderson recalled that someone at the hospital had posed the question: What if another war were to come and the hospital could not get enough people to staff the treatment program? What would be a minimal staff pattern? One suggestion was that things would be fine as long as there was a recovering person who would run the program, and a clergy person.

By 1959 Willmar State Hospital had installed a formal counselor training program, a formal pastoral training program, and a modest research department. By the time Bradley left for Chicago in 1960, the hospital had adopted a multidisciplinary approach to alcoholism and the treatment of it as both a disease and as the primary problem. Looking back at the early days, Bradley reflected upon the *esprit de corps*:

> I don't think our motivations were any grand ones — but we were able to relate with each other. We had an enormous amount of support for what each other was doing — one quarter of our time at Willmar was spent supporting one another. By our conversations — sneaking away from downstairs and coming up and locking the door, because you were trying to hide from someone else. It was always the same people who stuck together — all the people who came and went over a ten year period — the same ones who talked about the same things — or talked in a similar fashion.

For Bradley the decade was an adventure. No matter where he went — Willmar State Hospital, Hazelden, 2218, Pioneer House, or Patrick Butler's Summit Avenue residence in St. Paul — Bradley remembered the support and reinforcement he received. The spirit of that adventure was to cascade like a mighty cataract into the Hazelden event during the decade of the sixties and inspire what was to become the refined and finely-calibrated Hazelden model.

7. The Bridge from Willmar to Hazelden

THE CONTRASTS are striking. The events at Willmar State Hospital occurred at a time when there was great pessimism and even despair about the possibilities of recovery for alcoholics. Their high death rate precluded optimism. The social stigma surrounding alcoholics also enveloped the people associated with them or seeking to help them. Even the mental patients looked down upon the "inebs" similar to the way alcoholics looked down upon those who ingested pills.

It is in this social context and because of it that the Willmar experience became such a rich and rewarding phenomenon. Willmar State Hospital, under Bradley's leadership, began the process of raising the nation's consciousness about the rehabilitation of alcoholics, that they should not be stigmatized or looked down upon because of their disease. Humane treatment was possible when facilitated by a multidisciplinary team in an intensive treatment setting and in a caring community of fellow sufferers.

The Willmar experience was not an isolated phenomenon. As Bradley recalled:

> It finally got so that it was almost an adventure — to go to Hazelden, or to 2218, or Pioneer House. At that time we were continually reinforced. Everywhere we went we were encouraged.

A.A. was slowly but surely enriching the country with its experience. Pat Cronin was disseminating the A.A. experience throughout the Midwest and modeling A.A. based rehabilitation services at Pioneer House. Lynn Carroll was including Canada in his lecture itineraries, thereby providing Hazelden with the beginnings

Dan Anderson and Pat Butler

of its international reputation.

During the fifties, some of Minnesota's practitioners who treated alcoholic patients were sharing their experiences with scholars from the Yale Summer School of Alcohol Studies, located in New Haven, Connecticut. There was a sense and spirit of being at the edge of a new frontier in helping a major group of the helpless.

There was a central piece in the convergence of these fascinating events. Bradley said: "My life ended up between Willmar and Summit Avenue." By Summit Avenue, he meant the St. Paul home of Patrick Butler.

Starting with his own recovery in 1950, Butler dedicated his life to helping as many alcoholics as he could. Most visible was his sponsorship during the fifties of Fellowship Club, and Dia Linn, an alcohol treatment program for women, opened by Hazelden in White Bear Lake, Minnesota. Hazelden's high visibility and reputation was enhanced in March 1953 when Butler became vice president and director of the National Council on Alcoholism. He was also responsible for establishing and maintaining a close relationship between Hazelden and the Yale Summer School of Alcohol Studies, despite Lynn Carroll's deep distrust of Yale's intellectual and scientific efforts to help alcoholics.

In regard to the Minnesota experience, Butler can be thought of as the Pontifex Maximus, which in the days of Imperial Rome, meant the "high priest," or translated from Latin, the "great bridge builder."

Butler forged the treatment links between Willmar State Hospital and Hazelden. He made Hazelden the beneficiary of the hospital's expertise.

Butler's primary focus during the fifties was rehabilitation and how to make Hazelden the best rehabilitation center possible. He was very aware of Bradley's innovative style and Bradley's uncertainty as to where everything would lead. Although Butler was excited about events at Willmar State Hospital, he was primarily interested in Hazelden's future. He saw great possibilities in linking the private, freestanding Hazelden to the discoveries of and the direction taken by the state hospital at Willmar.

A keen observer of people, Butler soon intuited the potential of the young Daniel Anderson. He gradually came to believe that Anderson had the potential to span the geographical distance and attitudinal differences between Willmar and Center City.

In 1953, Butler invited Bradley and Anderson to his home in St. Paul for dinner where he offered to help finance their educations if they would assist in forging the future of the Hazelden venture. Anderson's talents and vision were subsequently tied to Center City. He completed his master's degree dissertation in Clinical Psychology for Loyola University, Chicago in 1956, while working on his doctoral degree at the University of Ottawa, Canada during 1956 and 1957.

Of course, Anderson also became a member of the new multi-disciplinary concept and team which was emerging under Bradley's guidance. Like all the professionals involved in the Willmar adventure, Anderson had to find his way. He encountered other professional psychologists who either considered the alcoholic a lost cause or who held the belief that alcoholism was merely a symptom of some other personality disorder. In either case, Anderson's ideas were suspect. Reflecting upon those early days, Anderson recalled: "All I know is in the early days of alcoholism [treatment], I was considered an inferior professional person working with alcoholics — and was looked down upon."

Moreover, Anderson had to discover his relationship with A.A. and the Counselors on Alcoholism. Among all the professionals, the psychologist was the most threatening to the A.A. counselor — both at Willmar and later at Hazelden. The integrating process was a difficult learning experience for both the psychologist and the counselor. Anderson and the other professionals would later learn from Fred Eiden that the illness of alcoholism was responsible for a great deal of the "craziness," the self-defeating and irresponsible behavior observed in alcoholics.

At first, the A.A. approach was mysterious to Anderson as it was to most professionals. But unlike many professionals, Anderson's suspicions made him inquisitive — a curiosity enveloped in genuine openness. His insights brought him conviction about the validity of A.A. His unique talent was his ability to translate the problem of and the response to alcoholism into categories that professionals could understand. Butler recalled:

> I remember Selden Bacon [director of the Yale Summer School of Alcohol Studies] sitting next to me while Dan lectured on his "Learning Theories," and Bacon said: "Where did that guy come from?" He didn't expect to see any experts there [at Hazelden].

Anderson had the ability to bridge the gap between A.A. and the professionals. He did this through his lectures at Hazelden, and over the years both nationally and internationally on the speaking circuit.

The changes Anderson was to introduce at Hazelden gained

acceptance due to the fact that he began to understand an alcoholic's reasoning. He was able to develop the right kind of empathy and speak the language of the alcoholic, whether in private counseling sessions or in lectures. These changes were to bring the best methods of Willmar State Hospital to the Hazelden environment. But in order to accomplish that, Anderson needed an experimental laboratory which would be found in Dia Linn, Hazelden's program for women.

No sooner had the Butler family assumed leadership of Hazelden in 1951, than Pat Butler went about forming a Hazelden advisory council to assist in educating business and industry about providing referrals to Hazelden. He solicited members geographically representative of all of Minnesota to be on a Hazelden advisory board: John B. Arnold, Duluth; J. C. Hopponen, Fergus Falls; Otto Zapp, St. Cloud; Archie F. Carlson, Willmar; Earl J. O'Brien, Brainerd; and, among others, Jim Lennon, Owatonna.

To assist with the purpose of the advisory council, namely the recruitment of referrals, Hazelden opened an Information and Referral Center at 2639 University Avenue in St. Paul. The office served a number of functions: a quasi-business office, a coordinating center for transportation, and an unsophisticated referral and diagnostic center. In reality, the office was a forerunner of the modern and sophisticated diagnostic, referral, and community outreach components of the continuum of care for chemically dependent people.

Hazelden's St. Paul office also served as an educational and informational resource, which eventually went by the title, Foundation Book and Library. The office and its library, which provided educational items for those interested in alcoholism, was moved to Fellowship Club in 1958.

Butler wanted the St. Paul office to also serve as a resource center for Twin Cities companies interested in having comprehensive educational programs on alcoholism sponsored by Hazelden. An advertisement appeared in the 15 November 1953 *St. Paul Pioneer Press*, with this caption: "What to do when trusted executives become drinking problems — Learn how the Hazelden Foundation can help."

This comprehensive educational program was a forerunner of Hazelden's contemporary employee assistance program concept.

In 1952, Butler hired Leroy "Bud" Murphy, a friend and recovering alcoholic, to convince industries in the St. Paul area of the need for a program to help alcoholics. Butler's pragmatic mind was again at work. He wanted to increase the patient population at Hazelden. "Hazelden had empty beds at that time," Butler said, "so my effort was not all out of great charity."

The response to Murphy's efforts was poor. He was lucky if he could get to talk to a member of a company's personnel department. Murphy's assignment lasted only a few months.

But Butler persisted and sought a more organized and business-like approach. In 1953, he asked John Cook, an industrial consultant who at that time was the director of Fellowship Club, to define a rationale as well as the goals and objectives of an employee assistance program.

A *Hazelden Plan for Business and Industry* was mailed to various employers in the Twin Cities with an accompanying letter describing the cost of alcoholism to industry. The plan was highly sophisticated, well thought out, and eminently credible. It could have served as a model today except that its target (what it called the "Hidden Man") was limited to the problem of alcoholism. The plan was directed toward both the hidden man and woman in the workplace. The plan urged that the labor unions, if they were part of an organization, should be brought into the picture. It recommended training by Hazelden, the selection of a qualified person within the business organization to supervise the program, the establishment of written policies and procedures, the use of the Hazelden Information and Referral Center in St. Paul as a diagnostic and referral resource, and the employment of Hazelden at Center City as a treatment center.

The EAP blueprint indicated that similar plans in place prior to Hazelden's "have resulted in marked reduction in absenteeism, a definite decrease in accident ratio, higher production, and a marked improvement in the employer-employee relationship." The Hazelden design was truly a precocious model, but this educational and consultative division of Hazelden was not pursued as vigorously then as it would be in the 1970s.

During the fifties, Hazelden's educational efforts were achieved in the following ways:

The *Hazelden Newsletter*

The publication of the *Hazelden Newsletter* in December 1952 served as a unifying and fortifying link for the alumni — the "parolees" as they were affectionately called. Besides being a monthly bulletin of events at Hazelden, the newsletter was also an effective educational tool that reproduced small articles and quotations to enhance and encourage the maintenance of sobriety. Both Carroll and Lon Jacobson (Carroll's assistant from 1958 to 1965) contributed spiritual exhortations and insights. Jacobson's could be easily recognized. He culled many of his ideas from the works of St. Francoise De Sales.

The *Hazelden Newsletter* served another purpose. During the fifties, Hazelden prepared and distributed thousands of pieces of literature, much of it free to the public upon request, concerning the nature of alcoholism and its treatment. A great many educational items were mailed with the monthly *Hazelden Newsletter*. One of the first of these items was a wallet-size card with the printed poem "Man in the Glass," which had always been in great demand. This poem has become one of the most prized pieces in tool literature (pamphlets, books, and leaflets that assist the recovering person in working the Twelve Steps). As the newsletter urged, "Man in the Glass" was "to be read when one's thinkin' is stinkin'."

A Diagnostic Test

Another item of significance was a cracker-barrel diagnostic test, a drawing titled *Progressive Symptoms of Alcoholism*, which in its simple format is probably equally as effective for the ordinary person as the scientific Jellinek Chart. This educational effort had a wide impact. The February 1956 *Hazelden Newsletter* stated:

> The fame of our *Progressive Symptoms of Alcoholism* drawing [which appeared as an attachment to the *Hazelden Newsletter* in June 1955] has spread to great distances. A full-scale reproduction of it illustrated an article in the *Durham Morning Herald*, Durham, North Carolina. They are in great demand at meetings and conferences on alcoholism. If you want additional copies of this or any of the other material we have sent out with our newsletter, all you have to do is *ask for them*.

Television Broadcasts

The employment of the media in Hazelden's educational efforts occurred very early in Hazelden's history. Hazelden authored a television series in cooperation with KSTP-TV in the Twin Cities for six Sundays in January and February 1953. The series was titled "The Hidden Man," and a panel that appeared on the shows consisted of Lynn Carroll, Judge James Otis of St. Paul, and the Reverend Forrest Richeson of Minneapolis. The *Hazelden Newsletter* delineated the purpose of the programs:

> If we subscribe to the idea that prevention should be the

goal of our efforts and that prevention can best be attained through education, then we should all help to advertise this series. [Also] the public does not yet realize that the alcoholic is a sick person, that he can be helped, and that he is worth helping.

Lectures

Another method for disseminating Hazelden's message was the lecture circuit. Previous to the opening of Hazelden, Lynn Carroll was widely known and respected as a powerful speaker on the topic of alcoholism and A.A. He continued on the lecture circuit even as director of Hazelden's treatment program. In 1953 he publicized the availability of lectures and movies. Two of these movies were titled *I Am an Alcoholic,* and *Problem Drinkers.* The accompanying talk was called "Tragedy, the Program and the Miracle."

During the 1950s the Hazelden rehabilitation staff, particularly Carroll, Zapp, and Jacobson, often went on extended speaking tours. The staff also began to participate as resource persons at a variety of local, state, and national workshops on alcoholism and the rehabilitation of the alcoholic. Furthermore, they served as resource persons and speakers at adult and school groups throughout the state of Minnesota. Toward the end of the decade the speaking demands were heavy and the strain began to show. The March 1960 *Hazelden Newsletter* stated:

> As you know Lynn [Carroll] and Lon [Jacobson] have been on a two week on, one week off schedule which, with a house that averages almost twenty men, is quite a physical, mental, and emotional drain. Both men have been taking speaking assignments which entail preparation and travel and are additionally taxing. Please be understanding if we are forced to cut down on the number of speaking dates we accept.

Publications

The beginnings of Hazelden's entrance into the field of publications were modest by any standard. Hazelden produced brochures describing its treatment facility as well as its purpose and process. The first of these brochures was titled *Guest House,* published in 1948 when the Center City facility was being thought of as only a rehabilitation center for priests. The second brochure, *Inspiration for Recovery,* was published in 1952.

But the great event that launched Hazelden significantly into

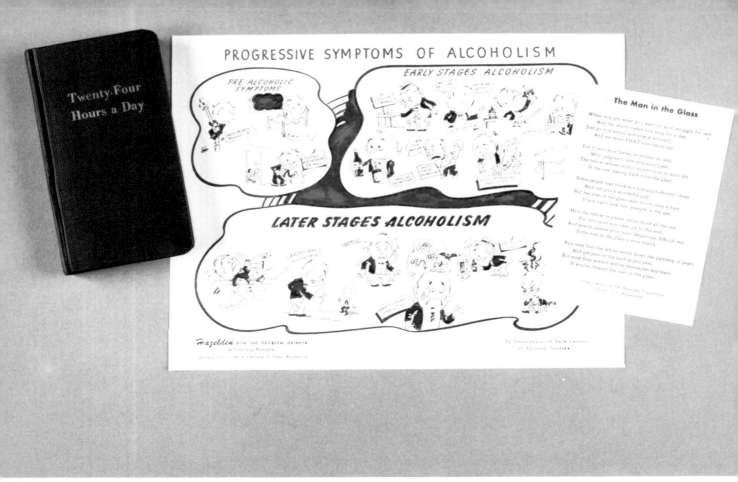

The beginnings of Educational Materials

the field of educational materials was brought about by Butler when, in 1952, he came across a small volume titled *Twenty-Four Hours a Day*, a meditation book for recovering alcoholics. The author, Richmond Walker of Daytona Beach, Florida, was publishing, selling, and distributing the volume himself. Butler offered to assume publication and distribution of the work. Walker agreed after the General Service Board of A.A. showed no interest in the undertaking. Consequently, in May 1954, Hazelden purchased the rights to *Twenty-Four Hours a Day*. Close to 5,000 copies were sold the first year. The book still enjoys an immense popularity. Composed of a short thought and a brief meditation and prayer for each day of the year, the book serves as a spiritual uplift for legions of readers. As Butler recalled:

> I did not realize the high esteem the little book has assumed in the minds of people until I went to a wake. In Catholic wakes, quite often you will see entwined in the hands of the deceased a rosary or a prayer book therein. In this particular

90

case, I was startled to see the *Twenty-Four Hours a Day* book in his hands. So you are able to see in what high esteem a great many people held that book. And it's been a great aid to a great many people — particularly a lot of loners all over the world.

Pat Butler had a comprehensive knowledge of the problems, needs, and potential solutions to the challenge of the disease of alcoholism. Wisdom and genius characterized his vision and activities in behalf of Hazelden. Possessed of a natural instinct for perceiving the whole picture, he was continually suggesting additions to Hazelden's continuum of care. His seminal vision of Hazelden's mission as being three-dimensional — rehabilitation, education, and training — fulfilled his personal and lifelong goal: "How can we best help the most alcoholics?"

As Hazelden grew, Butler's dedication and discipline allowed him to initiate the delicate balance between structure and spirit and to select leaders both astute and prudent enough to maintain that balance. He had an unfailing instinct for the particular and the pragmatic that were essential for Hazelden's survival. At each critical stage of Hazelden's history he was able to evoke Hazelden's potential for growth, not simply in terms of new buildings, but vigorous service.

To all who know Butler, he is a gentle, iridescent and affectionate man, rich in quiet strength, gracious dignity, great persuasion, and smiling discernment. To all who know Aimee Butler, she has complemented Patrick's vision of Hazelden with her own genius, affirming and promoting Hazelden's emphasis on the singular dignity of each individual who enters there. Her instincts for color, light, art, nature, and architectural imagery and symmetry have resulted in enhancing Hazelden's environment to the enrichment of the patient's dignity.

In a real sense Patrick Butler is the Pontifex Maximus — the bridge builder who spanned places and linked people, events, and ideas which otherwise could have remained separate and isolated a decade or two longer. Besides providing that sort of linkage, he had another quality shared by all great leaders — the great instinct of anticipation.

"Continued to take personal inventory . . ."
from Step Ten

8. A Decade of Growth — 1952-1961

WE LIVE IN AN AGE in which agency controls and bureaucratic legislation are pervasive. There are good reasons for this — to prevent the exploitation of the individual for the sake of profit, and to assure humane care and sensitive, sensible service. Due to the proliferation of rules and regulations, the problem arises as to whether the object of humane care is the individual or the system. The historical record demonstrates that, from the very beginning, Hazelden created an environment that removed the institutional aspects associated with a hospital. The record also shows that from the beginning Hazelden resonated with the belief in the dignity of the alcoholic — what made an alcoholic a human being, possessing worth and deserving of respect.

Recognizing the dignity of the alcoholic came naturally to Hazelden; it was not the result of bureaucratic licensure. Everything was done to provide comfort, cleanliness, and a caring ambience whether it be interior decorating, landscaping, or recreational opportunities. Hazelden could always be, for anyone who wanted it to be, a home away from home.

Environment

Hazelden was not an institution like Willmar. It was a small, homelike manor that provided an atmosphere for rest, reflection, and personal reinforcement. Carroll's report to the Hazelden Board of Trustees at the end of 1949 stated that the grounds were kept in excellent condition. This continued to be a priority item. The June 1955 *Hazelden Newsletter* contained this passage: "The Hazelden grounds are a spot of heaven. It is really most beautiful with the green grass, shrubs, and flowers." One thing Hazelden

The drive into Hazelden

had in abundance was an environment conducive to the restoration of the alcoholic's dignity and sense of self-worth.

Landscaping, the removal of trees, and the planting of seedlings, was an annual occupation. In 1960, 10,000 seedlings were planted, making a total of 40,000 planted since 1958. The rationale for doing this was simple. As the *Hazelden Newsletter* explained, "It is our plan to continuously improve the appearance and usefulness of Hazelden since it is symbolic of what men can do with their lives if they but try."

Recreational opportunities increased. A small putting green was added in 1954, and a horseshoe court in 1955. These activities provided breaks in the schedule when the patients were not occupied dealing with the more pressing problems of alcoholism. Even a large group of turtles in the patio pool were a welcome distraction since they demanded constant surveillance to prevent them from wandering off.

It was the little things that humanized the environment and enhanced the atmosphere. Flower boxes were made for the terrace; the outdoor furniture was varnished annually; and putting up a purple birdhouse for martins was a grand ceremony. The newsletter stated:

> Hazelden is developing into a game refuge. Wildlife on the property includes deer, red fox, raccoon, muskrat, woodchuck, and that cute little stinker, skunk. Among the birds are pheasant, loon, owl, lark, hummingbird, oriole, cardinal, and others.

The interior of the Old Lodge was given much care. As Jimmy Malm was the handyman who worked mainly outdoors, Nick Triemant (affectionately known as Michelangelo) became the handyman who worked indoors. He did the carpentry and the painting so that the Old Lodge's interior always sparkled with cleanliness and smelled of fresh paint. Triemant was also creative; while painting the basement, he marked out a new shuffleboard court.

Tasks were assigned among the patients so that the Old Lodge was maintained in a state of continual cleanliness. This had its humorous side. The August 1960 newsletter told the following story:

> Got a call from J.L., who perpetuated his name in Hazelden annals as the most unusual, if not the best, ashtray and wastepaper basket man we've had. This detail is a one shot a

Kitchen with coffee bar in the Old Lodge

day affair, snap job and much sought after. J.L. didn't see it that way; it ruined his day. So he'd start at 5 A.M. and get the dirty job over with, equipped with bare feet, morning beard, and no eyes. Customers beefed and even the help squawked, but J.L. stuck to his guns . . . or his ashtrays. By 8 A.M. of course, they looked just as dirty as the night before. What a system!

Coffee Cups and Medallions

During these years little traditions were woven into the fabric of the program which kept the attention on the human element and on the recovering person's role in becoming a part of the A.A. community.

The first of these traditions was the custom of presenting each departing patient with an A.A. pocket piece with "Hazelden" and "Meeting Time" engraved on one side, and the words of the

Serenity Prayer on the other. This medallion was, for the recovering person who earned it, a constant reminder of how and where he found his new way of life.

Another tradition, which started in 1960, was the personalized coffee cup. The motivation for the custom was not so much that each patient could have his own cup, but to catch the culprits who left their cups out and forgot to wash them — the height of irresponsibility! A fine was levied for each violation. According to the *Hazelden Newsletter*, the only people who committed a violation during the first three days of personalized cups were "staff, of course, who had originally proposed the idea."

Since the cofounders of A.A. believed that recovery came about through one alcoholic talking to another over cups of coffee, a new coffee bar was installed in the Old Lodge in 1953; this was enlarged in 1957 with the addition of new tables and chairs. It was so popular and the conversations were sometimes so long and so loud that soundproofing was added to the ceiling.

Patient Population

With the security and stability provided by the Butlers' moral and financial support, growth was inevitable during the fifties. The most observable sign of growth was Hazelden's occupancy rate. The year 1953 showed an average of ten patient days (the average number of patients at Hazelden per day), compared to seven in 1952 and five in 1951. The increase was steady. In 1958 the count was fourteen, and in 1959 it was eighteen patients per day.

Client charges increased, too. In 1949 the base charge at Hazelden was $100 for the first week and $85 per week thereafter. Ten years later it was $330 per week.

One of the major problems confronting Hazelden regarding patients during these years — the need for steadily increasing the census — was solved. Lynn Carroll was the principal reason for this. He gathered a great following and gained much respect. He was indefatigable as he pursued his succession of speaking engagements throughout the Midwest and Canada. As a result, Hazelden's patients came from more geographic locations.

In increasing numbers, patients continued to arrive as Hazelden's reputation for care and recovery radiated in many distant directions. Canadian representation was strong and prompted the request for a Canadian flag, which was donated in July 1956, to be flown at Hazelden.

Carroll easily recognized the importance of the alumni in making referrals to Hazelden both for the sake of Hazelden's existence and for the individual patient's continuing recovery. In a letter written in 1956 to the Hazelden alumni, Carroll provided some insights into the A.A. recovery process and the meaning of the Twelfth Step:

> I'd like to see every alumnus appoint himself an emissary of Hazelden. Sometimes we overlook the other man's plight when our own difficulties are solved. This is characteristic of all of us. One thing that is sad about A.A. is the men who, after a period of time, believe they no longer need to be active [in A.A.]. The full benefits of this program are secure when a man [becomes] outgoing and has as much interest and enthusiasm in seeing someone else living the program as he has in his own life. If occasionally we'd take an inventory, we'd find that we have been a little negligent in seeing that other men have the opportunities that we had.

If Carroll's observations seem too critical, in the same letter he was quick to note: "Another fact that stands out boldly is that each man who has been successful in his sobriety has been instrumental in sending someone else to Hazelden."

Carroll's cultivation of both the alumni and A.A. groups produced excellent results. In 1954 A.A. members referred 28 percent of Hazelden's patients, while 41 percent were referred by former patients — an astonishing total of almost 70 percent.

A second major problem regarding patients — keeping the patient at Hazelden for a period of three weeks — was less easily resolved. The problem of premature departure persisted despite the fact that Carroll reiterated to the patients that those who remained the full three weeks had the highest rate of success. In March 1956 the newsletter highlighted the difficulty:

> We have also known that "length of stay" is a problem at every place where alcoholism is treated and therapists . . . usually [agree] insufficient time is allowed to accomplish lasting results.

The *Hazelden Newsletter* then pointed to Willmar State Hospital's 60-day program and Butner's (North Carolina) 28-day program as being successful because of the longer stay.

Premature departure, coupled with tardiness of payments, prompted the Hazelden Board of Trustees to decide a cash deposit of $200 would be required, effective January 1955. This amount was later increased to $250 that same year. The next year a payment of $300 was required upon admission with no refunds for those departing in less than three weeks. But a significantly high population continued to leave early. This obviously had an impact on the other patients. As the newsletter put it: "When someone who can afford it [financially] leaves before his time is out, he makes those remaining restless."

Finally the ultimate step was taken. Repeaters were faced with a financial penalty. The newsletter stated:

> Effective 1 June 1956, anyone who has been at Hazelden since 20 April 1956 and has stayed less than eighteen days, cannot return without paying $400 and staying four weeks. Our length of stay has improved appreciably since April 1956. We hope this new ruling will further improve it.

Expansion

Since no long-range plan had been formed to meet the needs of growth, the existing facilities at Hazelden were either renovated or expanded.

During 1952, the first stage of on-site expansion occurred with the construction of an extension to the Old Lodge. Besides adding eight private rooms, the extension served as an admissions office and was a primitive forerunner of Hazelden's skilled medical detoxification unit. The new addition was affectionately named "Nightmare Alley." The two rooms at the end of the unit were referred to humorously as "the snake pit."

The addition was necessary because there were no single rooms. When a man arrived, he was usually quite ill. If he were placed with others (in the master bedroom which contained six beds and was known as "the squirrel cage"), he would disturb the other "guests," as patients were then called. Moreover, a patient who had been at the Old Lodge for a time and wanted to be alone could now request one of the rooms in the newly-built wing. Patrick Butler described how it was financed:

> My father [Emmett] said that he would pay for that wing. He was an old contractor and he had a great deal of fun supervising the work. But when it came to the end of the year and the bills were coming in he said: "Do you mind if you pick up the tab? My tax situation will be better next year and then I'll pay it back." That's the last I heard of that. He got all the fun and credit of building the wing, and I picked up the tab.

Hazelden boasted of its record that no one had ever been turned away. But as the years of the fifties progressed, bed space was no longer immediately available upon request. Lack of space was a problem not only for patients, but for visitors as well. Alumni, who were given a variety of affectionate names — "Hazeldenites," "parolees," "returnees," and "phalanx" (which, translated from Latin, means "army of soldiers") — took pride revisiting their alma mater for a day or several days. Alumni weekends as well as the Center City Alumni Association (whose members were mysteriously referred to as "BB's of CC") began in 1956. A.A. people loved to drop in unexpectedly, and semiofficial visitors made scheduled visits. Furthermore, the presence of the families and friends of patients overcrowded the already congested quarters. (Visits by families eventually had to be limited to Sunday afternoon and early evening, and finally to the present practice of Sunday afternoon only.)

The patient count was sometimes so high that Hazelden had to defer admissions. It was during these years of overcrowding that Hazelden grew beyond the space offered by the Old Lodge. Three other structures on the grounds were put to use: the farmhouse, the lake cottage, and the cabin-like building called "the schoolhouse."

The lake cottage and schoolhouse were not built for winter living and thus were remodeled for use as sleeping quarters. Central heating units were installed, but they often were inadequate to offset the Canadian winds and the snow swirling through the poorly insulated walls and windows. Patients slept under several blankets — sometimes with their clothes on. Once during a blizzard a door came unlatched and the patients awoke to find a foot of snow on the cottage floor. Legends, sagas, and myths, all with their own elements of truth, revealed the reality: Hazelden was growing and space was at a premium.

The increase in numbers strained other areas, among them the kitchen and dining room. The pantry had to be enlarged in 1958 to ease congestion in the kitchen. The following year a commercial-size stove was installed, and tables were added to the dining room.

The conference room was soon too small, and consideration was given to widening the room. Curtains were hung and folding doors were installed to contain noise and insure privacy.

Finally, Carroll had to acknowledge that Hazelden's hospitality was being severely strained by the increasing numbers:

> We've got problems of plenty! Our desire to have visitors is as great as ever, but our physical facilities are being strained — particularly the dining room. Saturday seems to be the

most crowded day, so please don't be offended if we can't feed you when you come to see us. Sometimes we may not be able to offer you a bed, but there are plenty of motels and restaurants in the neighborhood. (Special efforts will be made for graduates, of course.)

Thus, at the end of the fifties, the *Hazelden Newsletter* reported:

> The scenery at Hazelden has undergone a drastic change in the past few weeks. The old garage and the road leading to it have disappeared. The vine-covered fence around the tennis court has also been levelled, and the hole left where the barn was taken down has been partially filled. Most unfortunately the rains came before the landscaping was completed, so we will have to pass the winter with a good many things down and nothing in its place. The old horse barn is being transformed into a fine six-car garage and we started a new parking place in front of the new wing.

Staff

The annual increase in the number of patients also necessitated an increase in staff. Carroll's assistant, Otto Zapp, departed in April 1955, and he was replaced in 1956 by Bob Taylor, a businessman from Mankato, Minnesota, who remained a counselor at Hazelden until 1957. Carroll and Taylor fashioned a loose schedule. The *Hazelden Newsletter* reported that "Lynn will be on duty three consecutive weeks; then Bob will be at Center City one full week and Lynn again for three." When Carroll was on duty at Hazelden, Taylor would be lecturing in various parts of the Midwest. The schedule, however, had to be flexible as Carroll was often away on extended speaking tours.

Lon Jacobson was hired by Patrick Butler to assist Carroll in May 1958. Jacobson's sobriety began with his patient status at Hazelden in June 1953. Like Carroll he graduated from law school, but he never practiced law. His father was in the oil business, but Jacobson did not like that either. He felt an urge to deal directly with people. While Jacobson was visiting "2218," Butler offered him a position as full-time counselor at Hazelden. Butler would not allow him a few days to think about it — he wanted an answer immediately. Jacobson accepted; thus, he and Carroll were the principal counselors at Hazelden for the next seven years.

Jacobson complemented Carroll's approach. Carroll's highly polished, poetic and lyrical speaking style and apparent aloofness contrasted sharply with Jacobson's cracker-barrel, down-to-earth

Dave Kelley, Lon Jacobson, Bill Mill (counselor), Lynn Carroll, and Dan Anderson

approach.

Jacobson was scheduled to work two weeks straight and then to have a week off. Each working day meant 24 hours on the job. There was an occasional crisis, such as when Jacobson had finished an evening meeting and a patient went berserk with an axe, causing extensive damage, even to a police car, before he was subdued.

Dave Kelley, a patient care man, also assumed occasional counseling duties. In those days, patients were not assigned to individual counselors — all of them belonged to each counselor.

As what happened to Zapp, Jacobson received his experience while working the job by himself. When Jacobson would arrive to relieve Carroll, Carroll would tell him what Step he was to lecture on, and then Jacobson would be left on his own.

The schedule and structure at Hazelden had not changed much during the years since Jacobson had been a patient and when he became a counselor. The atmosphere was still relaxed and comfortable. Carroll did the grocery shopping, and he bought fresh eggs at a nearby farmhouse. According to Jacobson, Ma Schnable could still "spoil you one minute and scare the hell out of you the next."

Despite the snow and wind during the winter months, the temperature inside the Old Lodge was always "toasty warm." The patients continued the long revered custom of walking to the highway and back. Lights were to be out at 10:30 P.M., but the coffee room was always open for conversation.

The key elements of the program remained constant:
- attend lectures;
- conduct yourself appropriately;
- make your bed; and
- talk to one another.

The cardinal rule was: Never allow a guy to sit around and mope.

Every time a change was contemplated, whether it be renovation or a change in staffing, the cry was raised: "Ah, that's the end of Hazelden."

Carroll perceived the winds of change. Butler was continually making references to Willmar State Hospital. Daniel Anderson began his lectures at Hazelden in 1957. Both Carroll and Jacobson began to resent the arrival of psychologists and social workers as well as the ever-increasing influence of the Willmar experience. When Jacobson said that he might like to go to the Yale Summer School of Alcohol Studies, Carroll barked: "What the hell do you want to go there for? You know more than all of those Easterners." The entrance of professionals at Hazelden foreshadowed the ultimate conflict that was to arise in the early sixties.

This chapter ends with the year 1961. It is not an arbitrary choice. It was a significant year. There was unprecedented growth; admission figures hit a record high in 1961 with an average number of 21 patients per day. Even in those early days the literature division was showing a surprising profit. This growth was further attested to by an IRS audit.

The most significant event of 1961 was the hiring of Dan Anderson on a full-time basis in October. He was appointed vice president of Hazelden and became its chief executive officer. With him came the Willmar tradition and experience.

When Anderson returned to his job at Willmar State Hospital from the University of Ottawa in 1957, he began to consult at Hazelden every other Saturday, delivering lectures and providing psychological testing. The patients enjoyed his lectures (the women patients were transported from Dia Linn in White Bear Lake to hear them), and they particularly liked hearing the results of the MMPI which Anderson personally shared with them. Unlike the silence that greeted his full-time appointment in 1961, the *Hazelden Newsletter* welcomed Anderson in 1957.

Something new has been added to the Hazelden program. Every two weeks, Daniel Anderson, psychologist from Willmar, leads two of the conferences at Center City. We learn a good deal about our problems from Dan Anderson.

Carroll was not unalterably opposed to the professional at Hazelden. A quasi but unplanned integration had already taken place. Physicians were on staff (but tongue blades were still everywhere in the event of convulsions due to cold turkey withdrawal). Hazelden also anticipated Willmar State Hospital in its incorporation of another branch of professionals — the clergy.

Almost from the beginning the clergy heard the Fifth Step, first off-campus and eventually on-campus. From 1957 on, the clergy lectured on the Fourth and Fifth Steps. The addition of the clergy was acceptable; clergymen were the least threatening and their profession seemed to be a natural context for the spiritual catharsis that the recovering alcoholic needed and that the Fourth and Fifth Step provided. The part-time and subordinate roles of the physician and the pastor were not an intimidating presence and added a professional tone to Hazelden in its modest marketing ventures.

But the psychologist was another matter. His appearance at Hazelden was thought to threaten both the staff and the program (the possibility of a change from an A.A. model to a behavioral and psychological one). What had psychiatrists and psychologists ever done for alcoholics? Carroll had some sharp views about this. As far back as 1949 he resisted the thought of adding some psychological dimension to the fledgling program.

In the eyes of Carroll, Anderson represented psychology and the Yale Summer School of Alcohol Studies, both of which he felt challenged the purity of the A.A. approach to recovery. Carroll wondered aloud about Yale's intellectual research into the problem of alcoholism as running counter to Bill W.'s abdication of his sovereign, inquiring intellect in the matter of recovery — in other words, "letting go."

Consequently, from 1957 to 1961 Anderson's presence as a consultant was quietly tolerated but not appreciated. The fact that the *Hazelden Newsletter* took no notice of Anderson being hired on a full-time basis could have been attributed to (1) Anderson's modest and retiring nature, and (2) the negative reaction to the full-time inclusion of Anderson, the psychologist, as the chief executive officer of Hazelden.

Anderson was able to bring with him ideas and methods that had been tried and tested at Willmar State Hospital — a detoxification program, a primary care program, a combined aftercare and outpatient program, and a multidisciplinary response to a multiphasic disease.

Anderson had a program structure at the core of which was the A.A. program, and it was expressed in a three-dimensional process of communication.

1. Task-oriented groups conducted by the recovering alcoholic counselor
2. Informal, small, unstructured, and leaderless peer groups
3. Didactic lectures

These three methods of communication were already present at Hazelden in one form or another. Gracious sharing was the heart of the recovery process. Hazelden and Willmar State Hospital also had the same philosophy — the disease concept of alcoholism and the A.A. program for recovery.

New for Hazelden would be a formal assessment process; peer group meetings; individualized treatment plans; and documentation — the detailed records on patient progress. All were based on Willmar's 60-day treatment program. The formidable task confronting Anderson was reducing this to a three-week, and later to a four-week, program.

Carroll was an even more formidable obstacle. Jacobson's objection to documentation was a minor difficulty compared to Carroll's ideological resistance to what he thought psychologists represented. Anderson was aware of the resistance.

Carroll wanted a simple and unstructured A.A. approach to treatment. He had no patient files because, for him, records were a nuisance. Carroll's simple approach worked and patients got well.

Rather than risk a direct confrontation, the prudent, patient, and cautious Anderson made the decision to locate his office at Fellowship Club in St. Paul. Jacobson later reflected that it was the encroachment of this downtown office that generated friction.

In the chapter that follows, Dia Linn — Hazelden's treatment facility for women in White Bear Lake during the mid-fifties to early sixties — is referred to as a "laboratory." In particular, Dia Linn would become Anderson's laboratory to introduce, experiment with, and refine the multidisciplinary approach of Willmar State Hospital.

In 1966 Anderson would transplant the Willmar program, newly modified and newly adapted, from Dia Linn to Hazelden. His task was made easier by the fact that Butler wanted Anderson's Dia Linn experiment and concepts implemented at Hazelden, whose facilities in Center City were to serve as a new laboratory for further testing.

Lynn Carroll would have to accept it or leave.

*"God grant me the serenity
to accept the things
I cannot change . . ."
from The Serenity Prayer*

9. Dia Linn — Arboretum and Laboratory

LONG BEFORE the chemical dependency field's enlightened concern with the specific problems and needs of the woman alcoholic, Hazelden and Patrick Butler addressed those issues in the decade of the fifties. What today are heralded as innovations of the late seventies and early eighties — concern about the social stigma and self-esteem of women alcoholics, the idea of an all-female group process and environment, and recognition of the need for privacy—were part of Dia Linn a quarter of a century ago.

Because of the greater stigma surrounding women alcoholics, they have had a more difficult path to travel than men. While never promised a rose garden, the female alcoholic was given one with the treatment program at Dia Linn. And with its establishment, Patrick Butler — Dia Linn's "godfather and inspiration" *(Dia Linn Newsletter)* — expanded the possibilities of recovery for women.

In 1956, the Minnesota Advisory Board on the Problems of Alcoholism, chaired by Butler, believed the help available for female alcoholics was highly inadequate. Consequently, the board recommended that the Minnesota State Legislature establish a commission to look into the problem and report its findings to the 1957 legislative commission.

Rather than wait for the commission's findings, Butler and other Hazelden board members committed themselves to doing something on their own. They decided to create a facility where the primary disease of alcoholism would be dealt with in an environment responsive to the needs and dignity of women.

Butler first began his search for a suitable location in Minneapolis, but he was blocked by zoning and fire regulations. In St. Paul,

Dia Linn in 1956

neighbors had complained about the existence of Fellowship Club. Many residents in Stillwater, Minnesota were objecting loudly to the idea of a treatment facility for women located in their town. Butler and former Hazelden board member George Nienaber finally decided on a more isolated spot outside the Twin Cities.

Butler was unsuccessful persuading Lynn Carroll to set aside some acres of Hazelden property for a women's treatment unit. "They did not make bear traps big enough to keep them [men and women] apart," Carroll was reported to have said. As a result, in May 1956, a 300-acre estate near White Bear Lake, a suburb of the Twin Cities, was purchased by Hazelden for use as a treatment and rehabilitation center specifically for women.

The Arboretum

The grounds and facilities had been the home of W. O. Washburn, a St. Paul industrialist, and had been operated as a gentleman's farm. In addition to the main manor, there was a small guest cottage and two other cottages, all in excellent condition and ready for year-round occupancy. The setting and facilities were ideal for the treatment of alcoholism.

Butler, upon returning from a trip to Ireland, christened the farm Dia Linn, Gaelic for "God be with us" — a term expressing polite concern for the status of another person's health.

The facilities, ready for residents in July 1956, could house about twelve women. The minimum stay was to be four weeks for a $400 fee. From the very beginning, the woman alcoholic was assumed to have special needs and required a longer period of rehabilitation, compared to the three-week period for men at Center City.

In most other respects, however, the program would follow the established Hazelden model. Dia Linn's first brochure in 1957 described the endeavor: comfortable surroundings, an understanding staff, association with others with a similar problem, and the cultivation of hope and purposeful living without the crutch of alcohol.

The patients' nightmarish expectations of treatment were quickly dispelled by the soft beauty of the tall pines, the circular driveway, the fragrant flower gardens, and the beautiful mansion and the cottages. There were no bars on the windows, no dungeon locks or bolts. Whatever apprehension lingered gradually disappeared when the newly-arrived guests were shown the interior of the facilities: the cozy furnishings, the fireplace, the easy chairs, the television room, and the beautiful view from the bedroom windows — especially the view of the rose garden.

Nearly everyone who visited Dia Linn during the spring or summer months remarked on the rose garden. The *Dia Linn Newsletter* described it as "the most beautiful rose garden in the world." It was symbolic of the whole environment of Dia Linn — of the promise of recovery, of the delicacy, dignity, and potential growth of the woman. In the *Dia Linn Newsletter* was the following:

> We recently read "every rose is an autograph from the hand of God". . . such being the case we are surely blest with our rose garden blooming profusely this year.

Staff and Patients

Dorothy Borden, who Pat Butler had met at the Yale Summer School of Alcohol Studies, was hired as Dia Linn's first director. She remained only a short time and was followed in quick succession by Phoebe Brown and Hazel Taylor, making three directors in less than two years. It was a demanding and sometimes grueling job. A director was expected to stay 24 hours a day, and to be all things to all patients.

On 1 March 1958 Jane Mill became director and gave the fledgling operation a sense of stability and permanence. She managed Dia Linn until 1962 and then stayed on as a counselor until 1965, shortly before Dia Linn was reestablished as a women's unit at Hazelden in Center City. Mill's duties were manifold: she served as counselor and a paramedic, and shopped for groceries, medicines, toiletries, clothes, and whatever other sundries were needed.

The expectations were simple: proper behavior, performance of minor housekeeping chores, attendance at lectures three times a day, and conversation with one another. The heart of recovery would always remain the simple A.A. formula: two alcoholics talking to each other over cups of coffee. One patient explained how and why she felt the program worked successfully:

> Well, it's partly the environment out here, the long hours when you can think through your drinking mess. And the meetings in which we discuss ourselves and the others. And the Alcoholics Anonymous answers. And admitting we're sick and it's no horrible social disaster for women to admit they are alcoholics.
>
> But I guess best of all, we talk about our drinking, the silly and humiliating things we did. And suddenly something

lights a fire of enthusiasm in your mind. You say, "I'm not the worst; look at her. And she's going to make it and so am I." And it's that enthusiasm and gratitude for finding the answers that spurs you on.

Difficult Beginnings

Things were not easy in the beginning. The quick turnover of staff made management difficult, and acceptance of the female alcoholic by physicians or clergy was a rare thing. One exception was Dr. Cherry B. Cedarleaf, who believed in what Dia Linn stood for. She was a compassionate physician and made herself readily available, at least by phone, for the inevitable emergencies, such as convulsions which often occurred during withdrawal. Jane Mill became an expert in dealing with convulsions and providing emergency care while listening to Dr. Cedarleaf's advice over the telephone.

There were five beds in the main house, two in one cottage called the Doll House, and three in another called the Gate House. In the first years of operation, the patient count was low and the *Dia Linn Newsletter* was continually announcing available space. Yet, in those early years, the geographical distribution was wide, with patients coming from as far as California, Montana, and Canada, and soon all the way from Denmark and Holland. There were few treatment centers available for women at that time. Dia Linn patients who needed to be hospitalized had to be transported many miles away to a medical clinic in St. Croix Falls, Wisconsin. Closer hospitals would not accept them.

The Female Alcoholic

Focusing on the female alcoholic has produced an abundance of material and programs dealing with women's needs and methods of treatment. Today, a great deal of attention is given to the problems of women alcoholics, but the simple fact remains that chemically dependent women were neglected for a long time. If the removal of the "moral reprobate" stigma from the male alcoholic was gradual, the process of removing this stigma from the female was even slower and more painful. Even when the disease concept did gain acceptance, men were grudgingly given the benefit of the doubt; women, for the most part, were viewed as moral degenerates.

The number of women entering alcoholism treatment programs had been disproportionately less than the number of men, and treatment resources had been inadequate to meet the needs of women. Now, however, as a result of voluminous research, a

The Doll House and Gate House at Dia Linn

variety of approaches to the treatment of women are being applied.

Studies abound as to the physical, psychological, social, familial, and economic factors that demand consideration when treating the female alcoholic. The research also deals with the treatment of special female populations, such as the black, Hispanic, Indian, and lesbian woman.

There was a real danger that as the studies proliferated and the female population became fragmented into different categories with a multiplicity of problems, the original intention of the studies would be lost — how to respond to the primary disease of chemical dependency. Advanced research and technology have always had a tendency to complicate simplicity and confuse clarity of purpose. But, in 1956, the vision of the Dia Linn founders was clear and simple.

Female alcoholics had few choices for treatment in the 1950s: a psychiatric ward where alcoholism was treated as a secondary problem, or a state institution like Willmar State Hospital where the treatment of alcoholism was changing, though the institutional environment was not. Despite the liberal and liberating developments at Willmar State Hospital, there was still discrimination against women alcoholics, as Nelson Bradley recalled.

> And then we open the doors to women; but in reality we could never really open the doors to them. They were housed as mental patients ... we gave them privileges —

they could come and go. They had passes. But we had a real hard time selling the staff on letting the women alcoholics smoke. It just wasn't the moral thing.

As was noted in Chapter 6, a major step in the treatment of alcoholics occurred in 1950 when Willmar State Hospital introduced the "open door policy" to its male patients, allowing them the freedom to come and go and thereby distinguishing them from mentally ill patients.

The plight of female alcoholics was a miserable one. Despite the prominence, efforts, and influence in the fifties of such people as Marty Mann (known as "the lady ex-lush," who stressed to women the importance of A.A. as a lifelong commitment), women alcoholics were still a long way from being accepted. Local rumors of immorality at Dia Linn were not uncommon. Some people would drive by on Sundays looking for wild women drinkers. The sensational article "No Booze but Plenty of Babes," a title suggesting a raunchy expose of A.A., published in *Confidential Magazine* in 1954, found its later echo in the abusive rumor that Dia Linn was a den of iniquity and immorality.

Alcoholics Anonymous was not accustomed to having female members of the fellowship. It would be a long educational process before women were welcomed and not merely tolerated. Men in A.A. were asked not to sponsor women. Even in progressive Minnesota, many A.A. groups were cold to the presence of the female alcoholic. (The Northwestern A.A. group in St. Paul, however, was very warm and friendly to Dia Linn women.)

A further reason for the ostracism of the chemically dependent female was the fact that a certain elitism enveloped alcoholics precisely because of their alcoholism. People on pills were looked down on, and a great many women were addicted to pills, "goof balls," as they were called.

In 1958, the idea of "chemical dependency" had not yet emerged, and a talk by Dia Linn nurse Jane Cain at "2218" in Minneapolis only partially pierced the wall of ostracism surrounding the chemically dependent female. Cain's talk initiated the thinking that the term "chemical dependency" would better describe the Minnesota treatment model in defining all mood-altering chemicals; whether a patient was dependent on alcohol or another drug, he or she could undergo the same treatment process.

The Center City Connection
Gradually, the patient population began to increase. The word

about Dia Linn spread in a variety of ways: through advertising brochures; through newspaper articles; through women who attended various A.A. meetings; through conferences held at Dia Linn; through staff attendance at national conferences; and through the many interested observers Butler brought to lunch or supper at Dia Linn.

The Dia Linn alumnae were a great resource because they shared their experiences with patients over evening meals and lectures; they also served as sponsors and referral sources.

One night a week, one of the counselors from Hazelden in Center City would travel to Dia Linn to lecture (Lon Jacobson was popular). Starting in 1958, the Dia Linn women would travel to Center City every other Saturday to hear Dan Anderson's lectures. The male and female patients would have lunch together and share experiences. This was particularly fortunate as the recovering male patients would eventually refer women alcoholics to Dia Linn.

From the beginning, like the men, the women were expected to take the Fifth Step of A.A. They had the services of Father Nicholas Finn of St. Mary's Catholic Church in White Bear Lake; he had already been doing Fifth Step work with men. Women went to the rectory where Father Finn's sense of caring and Irish humor put them at ease. All, however, was not cheerful and harmonious: once a woman almost threw a paperweight at him because of his pursuit of the patient's honesty.

Gradually, other clergy became involved. The Reverend Phil Hansen, the Lutheran pastor of Holy Redeemer Church in White Bear Lake, would visit Dia Linn and assist in hearing Fifth Steps. The Reverend John Keller came to Dia Linn once a month to lecture on the Fourth and Fifth Steps. He did this during the dinner hour since he had to be at Center City for the men's 7:30 P.M. meeting. He was well-received by the women as was the recovering Episcopal priest, the Reverend Vern Johnson. Some of the best therapeutic sessions for patients were conversations over supper with staff, clergy, or returning alumnae.

The Laboratory

As was the case at Center City, expanded facilities and a more formal program structure were inevitable at Dia Linn. By 1959, Dia Linn had trouble finding space for all its guests. "You will be happy to know that September and October found us with a full house and guests in the cottages," the *Dia Linn Newsletter* noted. The result was that plans were made to add on to Dia Linn, and a new addition was ready for occupancy in January 1962. The capacity of the main manor now stood at seventeen.

The growth of the facility foreshadowed the expansion and change of staff, which consequently signaled changes in the program. Starting in 1960, a part of staff development included sending members of the Dia Linn staff to observe the alcoholism treatment program at Willmar State Hospital. And the staff of Willmar State Hospital came to Dia Linn to observe and suggest program changes.

On 1 July 1962 John Harkness, a clinical psychologist, was hired by Dan Anderson as the new director of Dia Linn. He had been director of the alcoholism treatment program at the state hospital in Jamestown, North Dakota. Under the direction of Harkness, Dia Linn grew: in September 1963, there were 23 patients; the cottages were refurbished and used to capacity by patients who were nearing the completion of their treatment.

With Harkness' arrival and under Anderson's direction, the nursing staff was expanded to provide around-the-clock service. A multidisciplinary staff was established — psychologist, nurse, counselor, clergy, and a social worker. Formal charting procedures were introduced with the use of intake forms, counselor notes, and nursing notes (in contrast to the use of index cards that would remain the method at Center City until 1965).

Patients were assigned to a specific counselor, and group therapy sessions were introduced. Every morning at staff meetings, files would be read and added to. Dr. Cedarleaf's somewhat casual and loosely defined relationship with Dia Linn was replaced by a clearly delineated consultant contract with Dr. Tom Briggs of the White Bear Clinic. It was through Briggs that St. John's Hospital in St. Paul opened its doors to women who had serious cases of withdrawal and needed hospitalization.

A daily schedule was introduced. At 9:30 A.M. there was a lecture followed by one-to-one sessions with patients and their counselors. Another lecture occurred at 2:00 P.M., and then there were group therapy sessions. Finally, at 7:00 P.M. there was a third lecture.

Every Friday afternoon and evening, aftercare sessions were held, bringing alumnae from nearby and distant places. Some Fridays there were as many as fifty returning pilgrims to share in their newly discovered fellowship and sobriety.

Harkness knew that a husband and frequently the children of an alcoholic became dysfunctional after exposure to the drinking excesses of a wife or mother over the years; thus, the reeducation of the family was an essential part of the Dia Linn program after 1962. A more structured and professional approach was accomplished with minimal resistance and hard feelings. Anderson was able to introduce structure, schedule, and the sinews of consistency into his experimental laboratory.

On the surface, these structural changes did not appear to radically alter the nature of the program. They seemed to be a logical and progressive (evolutionary, not revolutionary) development in the treatment offered at both Hazelden and Dia Linn. Although the changes were made for the sake of quality patient care, others viewed them as doing harm to the nature of the program and undermining A.A. concepts. The experienced eye could detect the change of direction by reading the following passage in the *Dia Linn Newsletter:*

> We are tardy in this first word to you in 1964. We have been steadily increasing the population at Dia Linn since the first of the year to full capacity and we trust that you appreciate that letter writing has had to take second place, as we believe, aside from the lectures, the heart of our program is the individual counseling interview with the patient.

The last years (1962-1966) of Dia Linn's separate existence in White Bear Lake foreshadow on a miniature scale the events that occurred later with much more intensity at Hazelden in Center City — the tension between the old and the new, the cherished and the changed, the unstructured and the structured, the strict A.A. approach and the modified A.A. approach of the professional, as well as the dialectic between two men: Lynn Carroll and Dan Anderson. Between Carroll and Anderson stood the bridge builder — Patrick Butler.

When the transfer of patients from White Bear Lake to Center City occurred, the women were apprehensive, the staff forgot the curtains, the men were curious, and many alumni and alumnae thought the move was a harbinger of Hazelden's demise. The good old days were gone.

The move occurred on Good Friday (some called it Bad Friday) in 1966. Twelve frightened women arrived, carrying some little token of remembrance — a potted plant, or something else familiar from White Bear Lake. They were anxious — a fear evoked by the prospect of change. They were also angry — over having been removed from the secure cocoon that had been their home at White Bear Lake. But soon they found the atmosphere of Hazelden at Center City the same as Dia Linn at White Bear Lake — a caring community, a home away from home.

". . . the courage to change
the things I can . . ."
from The Serenity Prayer

10. The Changing of the Guard

THE WINDS OF CHANGE were being felt throughout Hazelden, most noticeably in the need for space brought about by the increased census. Dia Linn had an unprecedented increase in the number of patients, from 86 in 1962 to 125 in 1963. The kitchen had to be completely refurbished, and five additional patient beds were added. Despite the increase, Dia Linn continued to operate at a loss.

The same was true of Fellowship Club. The numbers had increased but not the rates. The prospect of making money or breaking even had never been the reason for Fellowship Club's origin and continued existence. (The earnings from the sale of the *Twenty-Four Hours a Day* book were considered as balancing out Fellowship Club's deficit.) When Orv Larson became director in 1962, Fellowship Club began to provide more counseling, a greatly intensified A.A. program, and more professional psychological services. Fellowship also experimented with extending the continuum of care to having recovering people live together in apartment houses (known as "three-quarter," rather than "halfway," houses). Success had its consequences — the demand for available beds increased.

The demand for beds at Center City had become progressively greater. There were 505 patients in 1963 compared to 429 patients in 1962. The patient population had doubled within the six years prior to 1964. The need was self-evident. Every available space was taken; the staff, upon returning from an overnight stay away from Center City, could never be sure if their beds would be taken. In January 1964, a nearby motel was purchased; it was only five

Aerial view of newly constructed treatment units — 1966

years old, well constructed, gas heated, and provided ten additional beds to handle the overflow of patients, visitors, and staff.

The lack of space also prevented the adequate delivery of services, as Dan Anderson emphasized in the following quote:

> [Hazelden has] inadequate nursing personnel, inadequate fully trained staff; the need to transfer patients to St. Croix Hospital when immediate detoxification is required; the need for daily rounds of patients; lack of lavatory facilities; lack of counseling areas; inadequate facilities for food preparation; the disturbing effect of overcrowding on patient therapy.

The Changing Plans

The soundness of the treatment program had been proven, and now Hazelden had to expand. Because, in 1963, 31 patients had come from Milwaukee and 24 from Chicago, the possibility of a new facility in the Chicago-Milwaukee area had been considered, but it was determined that treatment would have been too expensive.

Pat Butler had already talked with the staff on 26 December 1963 about the alternatives considered for expansion and indicated that a great deal of thought had been given to choosing the most suitable location. The decision was made to use the present staff and buildings and to add new units as needed rather than to start an entirely new operation in another city and state. Plans were made at Center City to build four new units — small residential clubs — for use by both men and women, with a total capacity for 100 patients.

During 1963, additional staff had been found: Dick Solberg and Ted Wold as counselors, and Tim Sullivan and Bob McGoorty as counselor aides. Butler told the staff he felt the old Hazelden atmosphere would continue to permeate the new operation.

The decision to expand was a momentous one and there was a great deal of agonizing. Bringing men and women together was opposed by a good number of board members, staff members, and alumni. Early on, Lynn Carroll had refused to set aside a few acres of isolated land for a women's unit in Center City, so that White Bear Lake had to be the alternative.

Larger numbers meant new buildings. But would larger buildings mean fewer numbers? Would the increase in numbers destroy or lose whatever was in the "little black box" (a figure of speech, meaning the secret formula for success) that made treatment at the Old Lodge successful? Suppose Hazelden doubled and even tripled its capacity and no one was to come. Suppose the program was to be modified and it was no longer effective. Whatever was in that symbolic little black box was at the heart of Hazelden's success. Whatever it was at the Old Lodge — the small size, the familiarity, the intimacy, the freedom, the simplicity — it worked. People came, people were restored, people departed, people recovered — it was a simple enough formula. Would institutionalizing Hazelden destroy it?

Numbers and effectiveness — these were the issues. Hazelden was at a crossroads. The decision to expand was a risk, but it was in response to Butler's prevailing and preoccupying question: How can we best help as many alcoholics as possible? Despite the risk and many misgivings, the board approved the expansion plans.

The Changing Architecture

Serious planning began at the beginning of 1964. Hazelden employed the architectural services of Voigt and Fourré of St. Paul. Daniel Fourré and R. Michael Schneider, who was Fourré's design associate, were continually reminded of the Hazelden board's concern about Hazelden becoming too large, too impersonal, or too institutionalized. The architects were urged to keep in mind that the success of the program was in its small numbers and casual atmosphere. The decision was made to keep the patients in groups of no more than 18 to 22.

Today, a visitor's immediate impressions of Hazelden are warmth, light, space, room, color, cleanliness, and coziness. The architects were able to accomplish this despite many conflicting demands. They were told that although the alcoholic was sometimes very ill physically for a short period, a hospital setting was not envisioned; although many alcoholics were emotionally upset, a mental hospital was not wanted; and while many required spiritual help, there was no need for a church.

It was further explained that the atmosphere should combine that of a motel, hotel, and a residential club, but with a difference, to be left to the ingenuity of the architects. They were also told that space was needed for a library facility, for the use of visual aids for the lecture program, for one-to-one counseling, and for developing new recreational interests. The total conception was that of a therapeutic environment in which individuals could be exposed to small groups of other patients.

The architects' solution was to provide a small and intimate unit atmosphere while making the individual part of the larger community of Hazelden during lectures and meals. They con-

119

ceived the whole complex as a sort of "hill village," and described the process in a simple fashion:

> Each residence building, of eighteen to twenty-two beds, comprises a basic therapeutic unit, having an "integral form" and becomes a "neighborhood within the total community." The result is a cohesive architectural design that has form in itself and also gives form to the program it shelters.

The *Hazelden Newsletter* observed the planned building project as follows:

> We have been poring over the architect's sketches and blueprints for the proposed new building[s] . . . They look very, very good — like they "fit and belong" here. Chalet type buildings with glass from floor to ceiling facing the lake — downright beautiful! If we gotta use words like *motif* and *decor,* we have that too, but nothing in the plans to resemble a hospital or institution. We aim to stay humble but it won't be easy . . . [The new facilities are to be] for sick, sick people — without the look of a hospital.

It was a rainy Saturday on 22 August 1964 when ground was broken for the million dollar project. By December 1964, the footings were in place; and by the end of March 1965 the units were just about enclosed and thawed out to allow the mechanical contractors to move in for the first stages of their work.

The anticipated completion date for the first unit was May 1965. But the date had to be set back until October, and then again until January 1966. Delays in the delivery of materials, the Minnesota weather, and unforeseen difficulties (such as well-drilling encountering sand at the 300-foot level) were reasonable explanations for everyone except the "sidewalk superintendents" (patients watching the construction) who found that the monopoly on excuses was not limited to them. The newsletter reported:

> Construction on our new buildings started almost a year ago. Much progress has been made but completion dates have been set back several times for various reasons; like weather and delay in shipment of glass. While we are past masters at fabricating excuses, these construction people are no slouches either. Right now, it looks like we will be able to occupy two units (with heat yet) before the snowflakes come. Kinda puts a strain on a fella's serenity!

Two units (Tiebout and Silkworth, named after Dr. Harry M. Tie-

New units constructed using "hill village" concept

bout and Dr. William Duncan Silkworth, both early friends of
A.A.) were ready by January 1966. In April of the same year, two
other units were completed: Shoemaker (named after Rev. Dr.
Samuel Shoemaker, another friend of Bill W.), and Dia Linn. The
wait was well worth it, for it meant the patient-counselor ratio
would be around a comfortable and progressive 20 to 1. Old-
timers remarked that counselors would have too much time on
their hands.

The following article from the newsletter is a lighthearted, but
clear description of the buildings and their purposes.

A short summary on the new buildings: Work started on
two men's units west of the present main building (near and
overlooking the lake). Each unit [Tiebout and Silkworth] will
accommodate 22 men and a counselor, complete with meeting room, coffee shop, and multiple and private rooms, plus
many comforts of home (fireplace, easy chairs, and slippers
in the lounge). No locks — who could ask for more? Okay,
pipe smoking!

Two units for women [Shoemaker and Dia Linn] will . . .
[accommodate] eighteen women and a counselor to each
unit, plus their own meeting and coffee rooms, etc. Something new and important to both men and women will be
separate "quiet areas," consisting of chaplain's office, library,
and a large room to be used solely for meditation.

The new big main building will house important spots like
the kitchen, separate men's and women's dining rooms, and
a meeting room to seat 160. This will be for extra special
programs: we aim to include and welcome "grads" as always.

Also new will be the Infirmary [what is now Ignatia Hall] for the "real sick ones." Rooms [will] be arranged around a central nurse's station, with trained personnel on duty around the clock. This will accommodate twenty, plus doctor's office and examining room, diet kitchen, and painkiller equipment [withdrawal medications]. We think it is designed for tops in patient care. When the patient is well enough to participate in the program, he or she will be transferred to another unit.

The administration building is designed with ample office space, plus several private counseling offices for visiting clergy, staff, etc. After all new buildings have been completed, we plan to remodel the present main building into another 25-bed unit for men. We should be able to accommodate 125 in a little over a year from now.

The building years 1964-1966 were difficult from a convenience point of view. Unusual difficulties caused by construction of the new building complex accompanied the treatment process. The constant roar of trucks and machinery interfered with therapy and counseling sessions; wet, sticky, and sometimes slippery clay soil made walking messy at best, treacherous at worst. In the winter, ice coated the catwalks placed across excavations to permit access to other buildings; head counts were taken in the mornings to make sure no one had lost his footing and disappeared during the night.

The final result of the building project was an immediately visible one. What had been created was an extraordinary piece of architecture that preserved individuality and promoted congeniality and camaraderie. The new rehabilitation units graced its inhabitants with dignity, proving that a quality environment could be produced for the treatment of the alcoholic. Hazelden was to become an enduring testimony to the individual alcoholic's worth and dignity.

The Changing of the Guard

The years 1963-1966 were also difficult from the point of view of personal transition and change, particularly for Carroll and Anderson. While carefully nurturing its treatment program that began in 1949, Hazelden nonetheless belonged to another generation. These years witnessed the changing of the guard — old departures and new arrivals.

While construction went on, patients had to be cared for, and the problem of staffing was crucial. New staff had to be trained in anticipation of the increased patient load, as well as to replace the departure of key personnel in 1965. Finally, professionals had to be hired if the multidisciplinary approach, forged at Willmar State Hospital and tested at Dia Linn from 1961 to 1965, was to be installed at Center City.

Until January 1964, Dan Anderson's office was located at Fellowship Club. Although he was Hazelden's executive vice president, responsible for the total operation of Hazelden, he supervised Center City from a distance. Lynn Carroll, on the other hand, was director of the treatment program at the Old Lodge in Center City. With the decision to expand, Anderson was to become the de facto director of all of Hazelden, and his office was to be moved to Center City. Tension had been inevitable but bearable as long as Carroll simply commandeered the Old Lodge. But soon the Old Lodge would be just another unit.

In order to prepare for the added treatment services, Anderson set out to accomplish a number of goals: He formed a committee to work on areas of finance, public relations, education, personnel, and family issues associated with treatment. He requested that the board of trustees organize a similar committee to assist in these same areas. The board (in the process of rewriting its articles of incorporation and bylaws to maintain Hazelden's tax-exempt status) responded to Anderson's request by creating an executive committee to function more expeditiously in Hazelden's affairs and details.

Anderson chaired the staff meetings at Center City that included Jane Mill, John Harkness, and Dick Solberg, while Al Dauw, the new grounds and maintenance supervisor, and Bill Bailey, the business manager, represented the Center City employees. Carroll attended initially but his participation was perfunctory.

In January 1965, Anderson began to hire a variety of professionals to assist in the implementation of the multidisciplinary model. The Reverend Gordon Grimm would represent and manage in subsequent years the pastoral and training dimensions of the program. Eugene Wojtowicz would provide much needed organizational skills, and he symbolized the psychologist's "intrusion" on the Center City campus.

Until this point, Carroll had successfully resisted the residency of any psychologist at Hazelden. As his internal authority and control (not, however, his prestige and renown both on and off campus) diminished, and his participation in planning affairs lessened, a number of his followers decided to leave: Lon Jacobson,

Lynn Carroll, Lon Jacobson, Dan Anderson

Bill Bailey, and Richard Paddock, a counselor, departed in the autumn of 1965 to begin a treatment center in Cumberland Heights, Tennessee.

Jacobson's departure was especially painful for Carroll. Jacobson was very unhappy about Wojtowicz whom he confronted when the psychologist pulled one of the patients from a lecture to "read the Tea Leaves" (the MMPI) to him (Wojtowicz never did it again to Jacobson). The incident is symbolic. The old guard resented the formal staff meetings every day where each patient's status was reviewed; they also resented the presence of the psychologists (Harkness, Wojtowicz, and Anderson), and the lengthy charting. Jacobson said, "Lynn and I were mavericks — we did not want to keep the [patient] files." When asked what upset Carroll so much and triggered his own departure, Jacobson replied, "The encroachment of the downtown [Anderson's] office on the running of Hazelden."

Carroll would not stay at Hazelden much longer. Jacobson's departure and Carroll's passive participation prompted Anderson to appoint Solberg as head counselor at Center City. Although the Solberg decision was deeply resented by Harkness, who had expected to be director of all rehabilitation services, it was a wise move by Anderson who did not want to antagonize Carroll and his supporters any further by putting a psychologist in charge of treatment. Not without hesitation and some anxiety did Solberg accept the position, for Carroll was still director emeritus and his

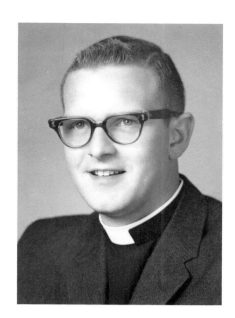

Dick Solberg, Harold, Swift, Gordon Grimm

presence commanded respect. But Anderson's mandate was clear: Solberg was to hire the counseling staff who were to represent the nonprofessional but core element of the multidisciplinary team for the four new units under construction.

On the one hand, Anderson was maintaining the Carroll tradition with the appointment of men loyal to it; at the same time, through Solberg's experience and training at Dia Linn, the multidisciplinary team concept would emerge at Center City. For the remainder of the professional team, Anderson would draw heavily on people who had been connected with Willmar State Hospital — Grimm, Wojtowicz, Harold Swift, Richard Heilman, and Dee Smith. Until her departure in 1980, Smith, R.N., directed Ignatia Hall, the skilled medical unit with its highly advanced detoxification protocols, which began operating in 1966.

Meanwhile, Solberg searched for recovering people who lived and experienced the reality, spirit, and wisdom of A.A. and who could communicate this through the example of their own lives. Solberg sought out gifted speakers. He soon hired Dick Frederickson, Bob Burns, Al Mehrer, and Reggie Stein as the first counselors to run the units.

Solberg was foresighted enough to see that the handyman concept (a person hired to do a number of things and to make sure things were in order) preserved at the Old Lodge would have to be carried over to the new units. Thus evolved the concept and reality of resident managers, or counselor aides. Their purpose was simple: they were to see that everything was kept in "apple pie" order, maintaining a serene atmosphere in the tradition of the Old Lodge.

While all of this preparation was going on, Carroll participated less and less in the changes taking place. He was disillusioned by the triumph of the MMPI. He felt alone and abandoned, especially with Jacobson's departure. His role at the Old Lodge was limited to weekends and even then he was frequently absent. His sense of loss was great, and in the middle of 1966 it was time for him to leave — not as gracefully as he might have wanted to.

Since 1965, Carroll had resumed his journeys through the Midwest and into Canada, reverting to his role in the forties and fifties as a missionary, preaching the message of A.A. But now he was no longer carrying the message under the sponsorship of Hazelden, as he had done so effectively before. He was no longer watering the roots of the marvelous and manifold referral system he had cultivated in behalf of Center City. To him, Hazelden had become corrupted and institutionalized by the professional psychologist. Many of Carroll's disciples also became disillusioned at what they considered the betrayal of Carroll and the abandonment of A.A. principles on behalf of psychology. It was a time of serious crisis for Hazelden. Carroll had a great following. The question was: Would this affect the number of patients coming to Hazelden? Fortunately, it did not.

One only has to listen to the lectures of the two men — Carroll and Anderson — to perceive the differences between them. Carroll was charismatic, while Anderson was intellectual, a conceptualist. They were not, however, totally opposed to one another. At Center City, Carroll had provided the foundation upon which Anderson could build. After more than fifteen years of operation, Hazelden had a rehabilitation process based substantially upon A.A., set in a dignified, warm, human, and personally enriching environment. Dan Anderson was welding that program with his own tradition, again based substantially upon A.A. but systematically and structurally delivered through a multidisciplinary method. Of course there were major and minor differences, depending on the viewpoint of the old or the new guard. The old guard saw them as major. As a consequence, it was time for the changing of the guard.

Ambivalence
Ambiguity → Conceptual
→ Normative
Wet vs Dry Conflict
Utilitarian Stress-Relief
High Risk Culture

*". . . and the wisdom
to know the difference."
from The Serenity Prayer*

11. The Years
of Communal Genius

THE PERIOD FROM 1966 to 1970 was one of the most exciting in all of Hazelden's history. It was a time of amazing vitality and erupting creativity, marked by a relentless flow of ideas and endless experimentation. The events that occurred during this half decade were guided by a group of dedicated, strong-willed individuals, diverse in tradition, character and personality, who molded Hazelden for years to come — perhaps for as long as it survives. All of them helped to make Hazelden the success that it is today.

These five years witnessed the following:
- the solidification of a clearly defined treatment program with a multidisciplinary approach;
- the creation of a short-lived repeaters' program;
- the establishment of an extended care program;
- the emergence of a variety of training programs, a research and evaluation department, and the tradition of the family conference (the seeds of Hazelden's Family Program).

At that time, all of these developments were linked to the rehabilitation mission of Hazelden (although Training would quickly assume its own identity). Accompanying this rehabilitative surge, the literature department (a subsection of the business office during this period) was giving signals that its own growth would be explosive (in the seventies it, too, would have its own identity in the mission of Hazelden). But the years of this chapter belong to rehabilitation, which stamped its indelible character on whatever Hazelden pursued in the seventies and eighties.

The Multidisciplinary Team
With the departure of the Grand Old Man, Lynn Carroll, and

Dan Anderson lectures to patients

the rest of the old guard, Dick Solberg performed his tasks as head counselor with more personal freedom and less external criticism. Dan Anderson was at his best in appointing Solberg as head counselor, making a recovering person responsible for treatment.

To prevent the development of the Hazelden model from being one-sided, Anderson created a Treatment Committee, which included Solberg, Gordon Grimm, the supervisor of Training, and Harold Swift, the supervisor of Family Services. Thus Grimm, a chaplain, and Swift, a social worker, were allied with Solberg, a recovering person, to serve as a model of multidisciplinary teamwork, cooperating at the very highest level of Hazelden administration. The alliance between the professional and non-professional and between Hazelden and Willmar State Hospital was formed through this team. Anderson was linked to the team through his assistant, Eugene Wojtowicz, who gradually became involved in everything that occurred at Hazelden during this period.

The trio of Solberg, Grimm, and Swift was humorously known as the "crash team." The appearance of these three formidable figures traipsing through a unit was the signal that a crisis was happening and they were there to resolve it. This was a primitive version of the contemporary and sophisticated conflict resolution process. Their appearances were intimidating both for counselors and patients.

Solberg (nicknamed the Gray Eagle) combined a strict adherence to A.A. principles with a great empathy for others. Totally dedicated to the A.A. movement since 1954, he came to Hazelden in 1963, and worked as a counselor at Dia Linn in White Bear Lake until he was named chief counselor at Center City in 1965. Due to his natural eloquence and charisma, he was in great demand as a speaker at A.A. functions. Solberg also directed the Counselor Training Program and was responsible for choosing the curriculum and screening applicants to work on the units.

As head counselor, Solberg's main goal was to establish and maintain the recovering counselor's prominence and preeminence on the multidisciplinary team. Known as the focal or primary therapist (whose duties involved direct counseling with patients), the nonprofessional recovering counselor was responsible for integrating the activities of the professional treatment staff of his unit in order to meet the spiritual, family, social, and psychological needs of each patient. In that respect, the professionals were under, not above, the nonprofessionals.

On the other hand, the Treatment Committee, which leaned

more toward the professional, had responsibility for the formulation of treatment policies as well as the evaluation of the treatment program. Thus, things were organized to allow for a distribution and balance of powers. Whatever the importance and impact of the professional, the lay counselor played the central role in therapy through personal involvement, communication, and confrontation with patients. He directed alcoholics to practical ways of being honest with themselves. Working with the coordinated resources of a professional staff, the recovering counselor's role in treatment continues to be one of the distinguishing features of Hazelden's program.

The recovering counselors were, however, often intimidated by the psychologists, who read the MMPI tests every Monday morning at the meeting of the whole staff. The counselors would listen, looking uncomfortable and casting bewildered glances at one another. It appeared that this was the era of the MMPI as the barometer of change, and that the psychologist was the program's watchdog, especially given Wojtowicz's powerful position. But the reality was that A.A. was the core of the program, and the agent of change was the Twelve Steps.

The success of the treatment program certainly lay not in any accurate prognosis provided by the MMPI, but in the channels of communication and dialogue — one alcoholic talking to another over a cup of coffee. Helping the alcoholic communicate was the essential ingredient of present and future change and day-by-day recovery.

The program's principles were communicated through the
- counseling session;
- lecture series;
- formal group;
- informal group; and
- the storytelling tradition.

This communication process was nurtured in an atmosphere of acceptance. The alcoholic gradually felt accepted by peers as well as the staff from counselor to housekeeper.

Lectures

The lectures, and then the films, furnished a thorough study of alcoholism and other drug dependencies as well as the means to cope with them. As Anderson observed, this medium of communication allowed the patients to sit in the lecture hall in an anonymous fashion and reflect on how what was being said applied to others. At some point patients would begin to recognize how it applied to themselves too. It was another method of breaking down the denial barrier. The counselors, led by Solberg, took turns delivering lectures on the Twelve Steps. Over the years, the lecture series was expanded to include, besides the Steps, lectures on the medical, psychological, social, and spiritual aspects of the disease of alcoholism.

The Repeaters' Program and Group Therapy

One of the outstanding features of the Hazelden model has been its reluctance to segregate classes of people or cater to special groups of alcoholics. Alcoholism is a very democratic disease and so is the recovery process, as well as the fellowship. However, Hazelden did single out the repeaters and those in need of long-term care.

It is no secret that alcoholics may suffer setbacks even after significant periods of sobriety of twenty years or more. Hazelden records showed a fairly consistent average of about 20 percent of patients returning for additional treatment. Special help seemed essential to them as their problems appeared more complex.

Early in 1967, special group therapy was established for repeaters four times a week. These sessions allowed patients to see themselves as others saw them. They came to know and understand fellow patients who also participated. Accepted and confronted by peers, patients found ways to gain a more realistic appraisal of themselves, as well as new ways of modifying old behavior patterns. What they had learned in the lecture hall was later internalized as peers graced one another with the simple gift of being present for each other.

Group therapy was monitored by staff members with whom the group members shared similar experiences. The patients' enthusiasm for this process was so high that the decision was made to set aside the Old Lodge (which served as quarters for staff and rehab workers) as a new kind of treatment unit. Just as Dia Linn in White Bear Lake, the Old Lodge became an experimental laboratory.

Many kinds of therapy techniques were tested, and group therapy was increased from four times a week to twice daily. Patients were taught to confront each other compassionately in a new group process nicknamed the "Hot Seat," later the "Love Seat," and then simply "peer evaluation." Alumni might remember that one of the lighter aspects of the process was that any patient reluctant to be constructively critical won the award of the "white hat" — the sign of the "good guy."

By 1968, group therapy and the group spirit became an integral part of the daily program. Many of the techniques learned in the repeaters' unit are now used throughout Hazelden. As the repeater population grew, it was decided that they could give valuable help to "first-timers"; thus, they were assigned to regular units. The repeaters' recovery even helped counselors. One departing repeater told his counselor: "During my first days here I thought you were pretty stupid and intolerant, but you seemed to have learned a lot since!"

Extended Care

In the same year special group sessions were begun for repeaters, another experimental program was initiated. Since the opening of the new units in 1966, a number of patients chose to continue their rehabilitation by working at Hazelden. Their problems needed more attention than primary treatment could provide in order for them to continue recovery on their own. While work therapy at Hazelden was beneficial, a more structured therapy program was needed. Another program was thus begun, eventually to be called "extended rehabilitation." Wojtowicz was instrumental in the development of this long-term component.

Space was a problem. The decision was made to locate the male extended care patients in the old Dia Linn residence in White Bear Lake, and to house the women in the Pine Cottage, a small residence near the Old Lodge. The group from Dia Linn commuted to Center City daily by bus. The extended care patients had their own staff — counselor, unit manager, psychologist, and clergyman — and the patients did reading assignments and participated in counseling, special group therapy, and attendance at local A.A. meetings. The length of stay was from three months to one year.

Ignatia Hall

An example of Anderson's intuitiveness for change was in strengthening the medical component of the recovery process at Hazelden. A 24-hour nursing service replaced the primitive tongue-blade approach to detoxification. A nurse's presence was a necessity no matter how accommodating were the doctors, headed by Dr. Marwood Wegner, from the St. Croix Clinic in St. Croix Falls, Wisconsin. Partly out of the need for a nurse's presence, and partly to involve the board more directly in the affairs of Hazelden, Anderson was able to establish a skilled medical unit based on high nursing care standards from which the Hazelden Board of Trustees demanded accountability. Thus, with Ignatia

Hall, Anderson was able to develop a more active board and provide skilled medical care for alcoholics and other drug addicts that was far in advance of its time.

Under the direction of nursing director, Dee Smith, and Dr. Wegner, medical director, Ignatia Hall began to use the outstanding detoxification procedures that prevented D.T.'s (delirium tremens) that many patients experienced during withdrawal. Smith, Wegner, and Dr. Richard Heilman, consulting psychiatrist, enabled this skilled medical unit to reduce the patients' length of stay in Ignatia Hall; at the earliest time possible, these patients were sent to the treatment units where they were capable of participating in the program of recovery.

Family Program: Harold Swift

Another important part of the Hazelden rehabilitation model that emerged at this time was the family element, which was intended to address the needs of the patient's family. To effectively respond to these needs, in January 1966 Anderson asked Swift to work at Hazelden as the supervisor of social work and family counseling.

After graduating with a master's degree in social work from Fordham University, New York, New York, Swift came to Minnesota to fulfill his commitments to the state for the financial grant given him. His first assignment was at Willmar State Hospital (1961-1963) on the alcoholism treatment unit where he worked with Grimm and, for a short time, with Anderson. His involvement — as a specialist in family problems relating to alcoholism — added another dimension to the multidisciplinary approach evolving at the Willmar hospital. It was not long before his observation and study of the dynamics of A.A. led him to recognize the importance of Al-Anon. He began to utilize that organization as an adjunct to treatment in order to facilitate the recovery of the whole family from the multiple problems deriving from alcoholism.

In 1966, about 45 percent and in 1967, 54 percent of Hazelden's patients participated in a family conference conducted by Swift. He soon became involved in training the staff and counselor trainees in the complexities of family counseling relating to alcoholism and other drug dependencies.

In the seventies, Swift was chiefly responsible for the development of the Hazelden Family Program which gained a national reputation as a preeminent model of services to families beset by the consequences of alcoholism. In 1985, Swift succeeded

*Harry Swift, Dick Solberg, Gordy Grimm, and Dan Anderson —
Treatment Committee — 1967*

Anderson as the president of Hazelden.

Influential and talented individuals from the Willmar tradition
were to shape Hazelden's future. The triumvirate of Anderson,
Swift, and Grimm shepherded the manifest and not so manifest
destiny of Hazelden in the years to come.

Research and Evaluation

The Hazelden model was working. The patients, the staff, and
the alumni knew it was working. What made it work? Why was
it successful with such a variety of people from so many walks of
life? A research and evaluation component was initiated to measure and study the outcome of Hazelden's treatment program.

As we have seen in Chapter 2, A. A. Heckman had proposed
scientific evaluation in 1949. Through his influence, the Hill Foundation sponsored an applied research program at Hazelden in
1969, with a grant totaling $182,000. The program had two
objectives:

- to coordinate all past and current research projects; and
- to implement a comprehensive study to determine the efficiency and effectiveness of Hazelden's treatment program, measured in terms of how people functioned following treatment.

Begun in 1970, a follow-up study of 1,500 patients was conducted at six-month intervals for two years. Again, Hazelden was a pioneer in this effort to determine whether it was achieving its corporate mission — to help as many alcoholics as possible.

Counselor Training: Eugene Wojtowicz

One issue dominated Anderson's reports to the board of trustees during the entire decade of the sixties — the lack of adequately trained personnel to serve the treatment division.

Otto Zapp and Lon Jacobson received no formal training. They watched Lynn Carroll at work and followed his example. When Solberg arrived in 1963, he was told to read the Big Book and listen to the lectures. Even as late as 1966, there was no counselor training program.

The beginning of a formal training program evolved in 1966 after the new units were opened. A few of the patients who had completed treatment and elected to stay and work at Hazelden to strengthen their recovery were on unofficial training status, learning mainly by experience and with the assistance of the counselors. But the counselors could not give them much time. Soon, other staff members — Anderson, Solberg, Swift, Grimm, and Wojtowicz — began conducting seminars with these people to prepare them for working in the treatment program. Then in 1968, through Wojtowicz's managerial skills, the lay counselor and counselor-aide programs became more organized and intense. Although the training program was directly under Solberg, it was controlled by Wojtowicz, a strict taskmaster, who was the primary coordinator for the trainees in alcoholism counseling. Under his direction, the counselor trainees were closely supervised in their techniques and methods for helping patients.

Wojtowicz, who developed badly needed and previously nonexistent personnel policies, shared the psychological tasks of the program and soon became Anderson's assistant, and secretary of the Hazelden Board of Trustees. In addition to supervising the counselor trainees, he was active in the training programs for psychologists and clergy. His position as Anderson's assistant, his talent for detail, and his long working hours allowed him to exercise considerable control over all the affairs of Hazelden — a control that created antagonism and suspicion.

After an unsuccessful bid to become Hazelden's director, Wojtowicz left Hazelden in 1971 to begin the renowned Edgewood Treatment Center in St. Louis, Missouri.

Clergy Training: Gordon Grimm

The Clergy Training Program, which was the responsibility of Grimm, developed about a year before the Counselor Training Program. Grimm had worked in the field of chemical dependency since 1958 when he was in training (and later became staff chaplain) in the alcoholism program at Willmar State Hospital. He received his master's degree in divinity from Luther Seminary, St. Paul, in 1960; at the invitation of Anderson, he came to Hazelden in January 1965 to head the pastoral care component of treatment and to train clergy. He eventually became director of the Hazelden Health Promotion and Prevention Division.

When Grimm was invited to appear before the board in December 1967, he reported that the Clergy Training Program had already developed an organized structure. The length of the training was three months; the first three weeks were spent in a treatment unit on patient status. The trainee was then integrated into the treatment team which emphasized the multidisciplinary approach. During these three months, the students met regularly at seminars and participated in intensive sensitivity training; they were required to read and report on relevant literature and participate in field trips, which included attendance at A.A. and Al-Anon.

By 1968, the Clinical Pastoral Education Program had evolved into a year's length, allowing for even better training methods such as group analysis of counseling techniques, role playing, and critiqued lectures. By 1970, 35 clergymen had been trained at Hazelden; in the seventies, the program was opened to women.

At the beginning of the seventies, a structured training program was in place at Hazelden, serving both Hazelden and the country. Anderson reported to the board that during 1969, nine trainees were involved in the Counselor-Aide Training Program, four were in the Counselor Training Program, and ten clergymen participated in the Clinical Pastoral Education Program. Moreover, one psychologist, two nurses, one physician, and one medical student also participated in training programs geared toward their needs.

Business and Operations

Internally, Hazelden had been divided into three divisions — Treatment, Business, and Operations.

Operations had to do with the grounds and maintenance work, under the supervision of Al Dauw, who succeeded Jimmy Malm who retired in 1959. Affectionately and respectfully known as "Big Al," Dauw decided to remain at Hazelden after treatment; early in his career at Hazelden, he performed a variety of tasks, one of which was to act as a policeman for the unruly. It was good-naturedly said of him that he would tackle just about anything: inside work, outside work, and the burliest and most uncontrollable of Hazelden's guests when necessary.

When the administration building was completed, business functions were moved from St. Paul to Center City and began to function more efficiently. One of the principal objectives of the Business Division at this time was to secure Hazelden's certification from as many insurance companies as possible.

The Business Division included the newly formed Publishing and Distributing Department in 1967. By 1968, 500,000 copies of *Twenty-Four Hours a Day* had been printed. During the seventies, Hazelden's Mission Statement would be expanded to include education (literature) and training.

Continued Growth

The units were full. The old Dia Linn facility in White Bear Lake had been sold and would have to be vacated by March 1970; it housed about fifteen extended care patients for whom space would have to be provided. There were other pressing space needs for trainees and for female patients (in 1968, one of the male units, Shoemaker Hall, was used as a female unit for ten weeks). An enlarged lecture hall was also desperately needed. Anderson suggested that the board might want to consider building again to provide additional space.

In response, the board formed a Project Planning Committee, and a development director was hired, Hal J. Peterson. Because Hazelden's debt totalled nearly two million dollars at the end of August 1968, a major fund-raising drive was organized to finance new additions.

The construction of the new buildings began in July 1969, and was completed the following summer. The building project included the following:

- The construction of a 316-seat auditorium, named Bigelow Auditorium, in honor of the Bigelow family, who had donated

Aerial view — 1966

large sums to Hazelden. This facility was to be used for daily lectures as well as for special programs and gatherings.

- An additional patient rehabilitation unit, with 22 beds, was completed and immediately occupied. It was named Lilly Hall, in honor of one of the original Hazelden backers, Richard C. Lilly. The expanding literature operation was housed in Lilly Hall's basement.
- A spacious two-story building was designed to blend with the architecture of the existing buildings. Called Jellinek Hall, it was named for Dr. E. M. Jellinek, a long-time friend of the alcoholic and a scholar regarded as the dean of research scientists in the field of alcoholism. Besides offices, occupational therapy areas, and classrooms, Jellinek Hall contained living quarters for extended care patients and students in the Hazelden training programs.

A formal dedication ceremony for the new buildings was held on 7 October 1970. Dr. Malcolm Moos, then president of the University of Minnesota, gave the major address, comparing Hazelden's mission to that of a university. Just as a university's function is to widen the options open to a student by education, according to Moos, Hazelden broadens the options and choices open to its patients through the rehabilitation process.

Shortly after opening the new facilities, Hazelden found itself filled to capacity; on 1 October 1970, there were 157 patients at Hazelden, with every rehabilitation bed occupied and an overflow of patients temporarily housed in Ignatia Hall. On that same day, there was a waiting list of 24 persons.

There appeared to be no end to Hazelden's growth. There was a time when visiting "grads" could sit down with nearly any staff member and pass away an afternoon drinking coffee and talking about old times. "But that is a luxury we can seldom afford at Hazelden these days," the *Hazelden Newsletter* stated, "because there is so much to do and so little time in which to do it . . . and it looks like those days are gone forever."

Patrick Butler wrote in 1970:

> In 1949, Hazelden was founded through the spirit and courage of a few laymen. Without their leadership and that of their successors and friends, the lives of many individuals and their families might have been tragically different. Today the treatment center that was fashioned without model is itself a model for other centers around the world. We pause at this milestone anniversary to express our deep gratitude to the founders and friends of Hazelden.

It is due to the talents, leadership, ideas, and compassion of many dedicated, strong-willed individuals that the period from 1966 to 1970 will be remembered as the years of communal genius. They were full and exciting years. Hazelden will never experience five years like these again.

*In the end there was A.A.
and with A.A. there was
everything.*

12. The Culmination
of an Idea

BY 1970, HAZELDEN had a total capacity of 167 beds consisting of
six separate 18-22 bed primary units — Dia Linn, Shoemaker Hall,
Lilly Hall, Silkworth Hall, Tiebout Hall, and the Old Lodge. There
were also 22 admitting beds on Ignatia Hall, and Jellinek Hall had
23 extended care beds. The Hazelden complex also included the
300-seat Bigelow Auditorium for lectures; a bookstore; library;
barber shop; beauty salon; canteen; exercise and recreation rooms;
meditation rooms; walking paths; and outdoor recreation facilities,
including a driving range.

By 1970, Hazelden had produced a rehabilitation program that
included diagnosis; detoxification; routine medical care; psychological evaluation; individual counseling; family counseling; spiritual
counseling; group therapy; lectures; nonroutine and emergency
medical services at St. Croix Falls Memorial Hospital and Clinic;
training programs for counselors, nurses, and clergy; observer
programs; marital communications workshops; and provided
speakers for A.A., schools, and other interested groups.

By 1970, Fellowship Club continued to expand and help people.
With a bed capacity of 37, Fellowship Club's average resident
count for 1970 was 33. The program consisted of room and board;
thorough indoctrination into the principles of Alcoholics Anonymous; limited individual and group therapy; and counseling on
employment, social problems, and job placement. The treatment
staff consisted of a resident manager and an assistant. The goals
remained as they were in 1953: assisting clients in obtaining productive work, contacting their families when appropriate, and
insisting that clients live up to contracted obligations and pay for
their room and board.

The Hazelden environment inspires dignity and serenity

143

By 1970, over 11,000 patients had been admitted at Center City for treatment of alcoholism and other chemical dependencies. The figure included men and women of all ages, races, occupations, and nationalities. Some were in the early stages — while others had reached the final desperate stages — of chemical dependency. Not all were entirely rehabilitated, but a significant number found courage to accept and profit from what Hazelden offered them.

The Grand Synthesis

Patrick Butler wrote in 1970:

> The remarkable spirit of Hazelden staff, with its blend of professionals and lay counselors, is a constant reminder of the hope that continues to characterize Hazelden. Through the years . . . the program has evolved toward a synthesis of the best known elements of treatment. The staff has worked with harmony and flexibility to provide treatment that reflects deep respect for one another and for the patients in care at Hazelden.

There are a number of factors that coalesced to bring about a grand synthesis. During the last half of the sixties Hazelden had developed a pattern of treating chemically dependent people; while this pattern of treatment would be modified in subsequent years, its substance would not change. Thus, by the end of 1970 Hazelden's status as the outstanding rehabilitation center representing the Minnesota Model had been established. It was a model that focused on chemical dependency as a primary illness, not as a symptom of another condition. The treatment was termed multidisciplinary and multiphasic, meaning that rehabilitation by a team of professionals and A.A. counselors involved treating all facets of the patient's illness — intellectual, physical, emotional, social, familial, and spiritual. For each patient, an individual treatment plan was developed to respond to his or her own unique personal needs. The process of recovery took place in a warm environment where there were formal and informal groups, relevant lectures, and bibliotherapy as well as individual interviews with counselors, doctors and nurses, clergy persons, psychologists, and social workers. Most importantly, there was time to think, time to read, time to make friends, time to relax, and time for two or more alcoholics to converse over a cup of coffee.

No matter how refined and sophisticated the methodology became, the basic principles of treatment remained the same: make one's bed; go to lectures; be gracious to others by listening, talking, and simply being present; and behave appropriately.

Hazelden never swerved from the principles contained in the A.A. program and process: abstinence from all mood-altering drugs, and changed behavior. The initial phase of treatment concentrated on the First Step issues of powerlessness and unmanageability, and on breaking through the denial that alcoholics carried with them. The second phase concerned itself with the individual's capacity for and recognition of the need to change (Steps Two and Three). The third and final phase dealt with the alcoholic's decision and commitment to change (Steps Four and Five). It took years of creative experience on the part of both the recovering counselors and the psychologists to incorporate these Steps into a successful method of treatment. The following chart serves as an example to explain the synthesis of Hazelden's treatment process and the A.A. program.

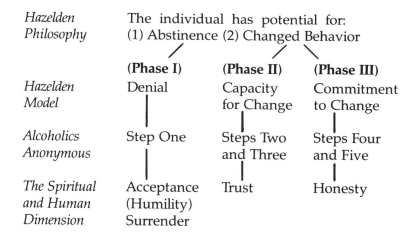

What also contributed to the grand synthesis was the remarkable cooperation that occurred between Willmar State Hospital and Hazelden. From Willmar came the multidisciplinary concept, a commitment to formally structured activities, a medical component, and the A.A. program and process. From Hazelden came the environment that could respond to the dignity of each male and female alcoholic — an informal, noninstitutional, family-like approach, and a strong commitment to the recovering counselor, A.A., and lectures on the Steps. Both Hazelden and Willmar State Hospital were committed to the proposition that all alcoholics could be rehabilitated, and both contributed to Hazelden's title: "The House of Miracles."

A New Synthesis

The year 1970 marked the end of one synthesis and the beginning of another. In one sense, the genius that marks Hazelden's rehabilitation services and created its unique continuum of care in a residential setting had expended itself. Nonetheless, the principles governing the pattern of treatment — the principle of a caring community, the principle of a commitment to teamwork, as well as other principles — not only gave the rehabilitation program lasting significance, but also sought to permeate the other emerging corporate ventures of the Hazelden Foundation.

Quality of care rather than profit remained the motive. A sense of family and familiarity was perpetuated. Lynn Carroll's prediction that rehabilitation could never work in the large and cold complex of new buildings was an unfulfilled prophecy, most probably because the new buildings were broken down into small family-like units — exuding warmth, trust, and familiarity.

The decade of the sixties was a time of innovation and entrepreneurship, a time of identifying a pattern of corporate direction, and, through rehabilitation, a time of continued fulfillment of Hazelden's corporate culture and heritage: "How can we best help the most alcoholics?"

In contrast to the seventies, the sixties had a great deal of informal communication. Soon, a goal was made to provide some structure and direction. In 1971, the board was reorganized; Patrick Butler became president and director of Hazelden. A plan was set in motion to merge the three divisions of Treatment, Business, and Operations into two divisions: Administrative Services, and Rehabilitation. Moreover, by the mid-seventies the mission statement would be expanded to include Education and Training.

Two characteristics emerged after 1970 that aptly describe the source of Hazelden's influence, which can be seen in its roles as a *paradigm* and as a *pioneer*.

The word *paradigm* is meant to describe Hazelden's power as a model of the various components of a continuum of care for the community, whether it be local, national, or international. Hazelden's influence and impact in the seventies derived from the fact that its rehabilitation process continued to be replicated as a time-tested, valid, and reliable model of care.

The word *pioneer* refers to Hazelden's pioneering efforts in disseminating the best ideas in the field of chemical dependency — ideas and information about prevention, intervention, rehabilitation, and health promotion.

Harry Swift, Dan Anderson, Gordy Grimm

In 1971, two important figures departed: Eugene Wojtowicz, who left for St. Louis to begin the Edgewood Treatment Center, and Richard Solberg, who became director of treatment at St. John's Hospital in St. Paul. As a result, two people emerged as dominant forces at Hazelden in the seventies: Harold Swift and Gordon Grimm. Together with Daniel Anderson, they became the triumvirate that charted Hazelden's corporate course in subsequent years.

In 1970 Anderson wrote:

> Centers like Hazelden just don't happen. From the founders has come a spirit of cooperation and concern. In the same spirit, the staff has carried on the work of treatment, training, and research, evolving into an effective unit for the arrest of alcoholism. And a very special family spirit, through the leadership of a very special family, has engendered an atmosphere of trust and love.

What is the reason for Hazelden's success? In 1978, 3M indicated an interest in purchasing Hazelden. One of Minnesota's most successful corporations, 3M conducted a number of audits of Hazelden and concluded that it was an organization with great strength, stability, and success. One of the 3M executives asked Anderson what was in the "little black box" that made Hazelden so successful.

147

*"Having had a spiritual
awakening as the result
of these steps . . ."*
from Step Twelve

13. A Spiritual Odyssey

AS THE PREVIOUS chapters indicate, Hazelden's growth is predicated upon belief in the principle of change — that Hazelden, through its staff, has the potential to change. It is this principle that makes the rehabilitation process effective — a life of sobriety is out of the question without the ongoing change from self-defeating behavior to responsible behavior.

The human condition testifies to the experience that the signals and even the thought of change can be terrifying. Every time Hazelden was confronted with change, despite its principles, it exhibited uneasiness. The prospect of change evoked outcry from those who lamented the break with the past, with tradition, with principle. The decision that meant the transfer of Dia Linn to Center City was seen as catastrophic and the inevitable demise of Hazelden. Catastrophic also was the changing of the Guard. Less earthshaking but just as evocative of hue and cry was the loss of the Old Lodge to the stealthy encroachment of progress.

There is always a legitimate fear of change. At no time was this stronger than when Hazelden undertook major building expansion. The reason for the fear was the prospect of losing something essential from the treatment process. The problem can be described with the use of a figurative phrase called the "little black box."

Board members and staff dreaded the possibility that, in the course of making the sweeping change from the Old Lodge to the new complex, something in the little black box that assisted people in getting well would be lost. Suppose that ingredient, the elixir, escaped from the little black box because Hazelden became too large, too impersonal, too institutionalized, too psychologized. Suppose what was in the box ceased to pulsate and vivify. It was not an unfounded fear.

I strongly believe the *spiritual dimension* of the treatment process dwells in that little black box, which Hazelden has managed to preserve. Because of that preservation and allegiance, Hazelden continues to be successful in helping people to recover.

The history of Hazelden is but another simple chapter in the ongoing history of the spirituality of A.A. Hazelden's mission is the restoration of the self-worth, dignity, and humanity of each and every individual who seeks its help. In that perspective, Hazelden's mission is the restoration and renewal of a person's spirituality. To be truly human is to be truly spiritual; to be truly spiritual is to be truly human.

From one perspective, a spiritual awakening, which is what Hazelden fosters and encourages, is related to change. To change is to grow, and to change often is to progress spiritually.

Because alcoholism is a spiritual illness, it requires a spiritual remedy. The Twelfth Step of A.A. speaks of a "spiritual awakening." Hazelden has been intimately associated with the A.A. movement and to the concept and reality of a spiritual awakening. Although it may be risky and audacious to associate Hazelden's success with a purpose so seemingly vague as a spiritual awakening, this association as an indicator of success merits consideration.

One of the reasons it is presumptuous to define the spirituality of the A.A. program is that any serious question about it evokes various responses. All responses are valid — symbolic of and a testimony to the richness of the A.A. program. The temptation is to define rather than describe, to circumscribe rather than free from traditional boundaries, to restrict understanding and application rather than liberate from accepted categories.

On occasion, Hazelden and its more enlightened and tested staff could not resist this temptation. For example, Eugene Wojtowicz rewrote the June 1968 *Hazelden Newsletter* at least ten times. He wanted to be very precise and correct in what he wrote regarding Hazelden's emphasis on the spiritual aspect of the treatment process. He stated that Daniel Anderson's first major goal as director of Hazelden was to strengthen the spiritual part of the program, which was done by increasing the clergy staff

> who are available for spiritual counseling as the patient wishes and requires. Each patient at Hazelden speaks with a clergyman at least once during his or her stay here.

Despite his caution, Wojtowicz was unintentionally misleading and misled. He fell into the subtle trap of defining A.A. spirituality by compartmentalizing it to clerical parameters. The point is not to diminish or devalue the role of the pastor as part of the multi-disciplinary team, but to clarify that the understanding of A.A. spirituality should not be confined to specific Steps. To separate spirituality from any of the Steps diminishes the fullness and strength of A.A. spirituality.

Some like to make a case for A.A. being a religious movement, pointing to its meetings as liturgical celebrations, its coffee ritual as a sacrament, its sponsorship and Twelfth Stepping as mission-ary endeavors, and its Big Book as a Bible. Such comparisons are totally misleading. While religion and spirituality do share some-thing in common, the fact that A.A. is a spiritual, not a religious program, sounds a precautionary warning and perennial truth. A.A. is not a belief in dogmatic pronouncements, in what a person must believe. Nor is it a commitment to commandments upon which a person must act. Nor is it an allegiance to an institutional church that a person must obey. A spiritual experience should not be confined to the parameters of an intellectual awakening or moral conversion, just as A.A.'s spirituality should not be de-scribed by the contents of one Step.

The A.A. movement avoids dogma, rules, customs, writings, and revelations that seek to inform and direct people in the ways and long-term intentions of God. A.A. shuns what religions often tend to be: authoritative, organized, and denominational. A.A. habitually avoids what the practice of religion often aims at: perfection.

Father Leo Booth, a noted writer on spirituality and addiction, has said that some recovering people experience the "spiritual awakening" in their lives by being led back to their childhood religion.

> Others speak of a "religious conversion" and enthusiasti-cally share as much at their local meetings. Still others remain healthy agnostics trusting in the power of the group.

Such a variety of experiences prevent A.A. from becoming exclu-sive or denominational.

While it is easy to describe what A.A. spirituality is not — not a religious movement, not limited to taking the Fifth Step with a clergy person, not limited to the Eleventh prayer Step — it is not easy to describe what it is.

Milton Maxwell, former director of Rutgers University Summer School of Alcohol Studies, wrote:

. . . we are in a better position to appreciate A.A.'s strengths as a *lay* phenomenon. And it *is* thoroughly a lay operation. It speaks its own lay language. It looks at alcoholism through the eyes of alcoholics themselves. Furthermore, learning from their own experiences, they have fashioned a lay society with unusual potency.

The following is one way of looking at what underlies the phenomenon of A.A. spirituality.

A key to spirituality is in the word and concept of *wholeness.* The psychologist Carl Jung had written to Bill W. about his own experiences in working with alcoholics, saying that alcoholism is a spiritual disease at the root of which is the instinct or drive for wholeness. Spirituality is the identification with that which is the deepest, most profound, and permanent element of being human. The chemically dependent person needs this unadulterated type of spirituality, having profoundly experienced a lack of wholeness, a fragmentation, a fracturing, a disintegration, a going to pieces; thus, the addict cries out desperately for wholeness, for healing and mending, and for integration and integrity. It is a life or death choice. For the A.A. person, it is a matter of survival. Wholeness, integration, and integrity are splendid words to describe the object of humankind's spiritual odyssey.

The quest for wholeness is present in everyone's life. Everybody has the power, when continually challenged through crises, to develop positive attitudes, to have healthy relationships, and to fulfill expectations. We are conscious of this capacity we have to bring all the dimensions of our lives — the social, emotional, cognitive, physical, and spiritual — into a unified whole.

Making sense of our humanity and unifying our total being is a normal process that allows us to develop into who we are and what we are about. Part of maturing is being capable of challenging ourselves and accepting challenges from others; in our lives, these challenges are called crises (or critical junctures) that will result in either generative growth or degeneration.

One dimension of wholeness is any person's continuing efforts to reconcile personal beliefs and values with personal behavior. In the world of chemical dependency, a lack of wholeness and integration results from the discrepancy between the values and principles a fundamentally good human being professes and the way that same person acts — caught up in the powerlessness of chemical dependency. For the practicing addict, the gap widens as the disease eats at self-respect and self-worth. The actions perpetrated under the powerlessness of chemicals creates shame, humiliation, and guilt — causing one to question one's effectiveness as a human being, leading to the refrain: "It would be better if I were dead."

The addiction process comes full circle as the addict resorts to a variety of manipulative behaviors and activities that increase self-reproach and leads to further disintegration. Lying and cheating become the accepted norms of behavior. The personal stories from the Big Book provide examples of this degenerative behavior. The double disintegration of self-loathing and loss of relationships is a contradiction of human growth.

It is particularly in the loss and restoration of relationships that the addiction process and spirituality becomes an intriguing example of human spirituality and models the spiritual themes — death and rising, and strength through weakness — of many religions.

Addiction and recovery can be viewed as two spiraling movements, one downward and one upward; both are essential parts of a spiritual journey. What an addict experiences in the downward spiral is a total lack of being in touch with oneself, with others, and with a Higher Power. An addiction can be defined as a pathological relationship of trust and love with an object or event instead of with oneself, others, and a Higher Power. Although this destructive process can result in death, it contains the seeds of an upward, vivifying spiral which transforms and restores the relationships previously lost to the friendship of the chemical. Negative spirituality can either overwhelm or be replaced by a positive spirituality that integrates and leads to wholeness.

The downward spiral is a "rending" process. Almost literally, the chemically dependent person is being torn to pieces and torn from the intimacy of relationships with others. The chemical is substituted for the human relationships that give meaning to life.

The upward spiral is a threefold healing process:
- *mend*ing ourselves
- making a*mend*s to others
- com*mend*ing a Higher Power

The Twelve Steps emphasize the resoration of relationships with oneself, with others, and with a Higher Power. That is why Hazelden emphasizes all of the Twelve Steps and the principle of dialogue — one alcoholic talking to another over a cup of coffee —to initiate relationships.

A.A. provides a program and process capable of redeeming

growth for chemically dependent people; thus, A.A. resonates powerfully with the potential of our human nature. Because A.A. deals with the central issues of life — how one should live as a human being, how the recovering addict should act, react, and grow — the program of A.A. is completely spiritual, equally as effective for the humanist as for those who trust in a transcendent power communicating through A.A.

I believe Hazelden's rehabilitation programs are successful because they neither compromise the presentation of the A.A. program and process and its spirituality nor cater to those who overlook, ridicule, or simply do not understand A.A.

A remarkable change occurs in practically all the patients who come through Hazelden; a conversion is visible whether it is physical, emotional, intellectual, social, or transcendental — or all of these. Any of these categories has spiritual implications in terms of wholeness and intimacy. Bill W. emphasized the spiritual in describing his own recovery.

> Conversion does alter motivation and does semiautomatically enable a person to be and do the formerly impossible. It was significant that marked conversion experiences came mostly to individuals who knew complete defeat in a controlling area of life. The book *[Varieties of Religious Experience* by William James] certainly showed variety. But whether these experiences were bright or dim, cataclysmic or gradual, conversions did have a common denominator. They utterly changed people.

I have referred to Hazelden as a graceful place, full of gracious people. The act of one person talking to another — the group process — is a gracious act. The formula for recovery is that people are gracious. In recovery or in the A.A. process, people grace one another — they give one another the gift of being present, of talking, of listening to one another. These are simple gifts, but the program was meant to keep it simple. The recovering person has a great redemptive power — a power to liberate others by sharing themselves. Hazelden's grace is that it keeps this redemptive tradition alive and is gracious to everyone who enters its doors.

Not content with simply recognizing that something could be done for alcoholics, Hazelden has pioneered and preserved a positive way of doing something for the whole person. It has been no small contribution — and that is why this history of Hazelden is titled *A Spiritual Odyssey.*

". . . and to practice these principles in all our affairs."
from Step Twelve

14. A Continuing Spiritual Odyssey

HAZELDEN'S SPIRITUAL ODYSSEY did not end in 1970 when the Hazelden model as a powerful formula for recovery was in place. This chapter is about the unfolding of events at Hazelden after 1970; this unfolding occurred in a variety of ways that may seem bewildering to Hazelden admirers and unsettling to alumni.

In the early eighties Patrick Butler suggested a striking analogy. "Recovery from chemical dependency is a lifelong process." As a spiritual odyssey, recovery "begins with struggle and is marked by continuous change, growth, and more struggle." Similarly, Hazelden's odyssey as an organization is intimately, manifestly, and vicariously bound to the recovery process. "Struggle, change, and growth occur on the conceptual level of theories, policies, and plans, and on the structural level of methods, programs, and organizations," Butler stated. Struggle, change, and growth as the ingredients of a spiritual odyssey are equally applicable to the organization as well as to the individual.

Hazelden's expansion after 1970 was fourfold.
1. Philosophical — Hazelden's mission
2. Internal — Hazelden's organizational structure
3. External — Hazelden's buildings
4. Dynamic — Hazelden's creation of new services

HAZELDEN'S MISSION

During the late seventies and early eighties, Hazelden's mission began to be debated. Should Hazelden widen its course or strictly maintain effective services for chemically dependent people? In other words, should Hazelden's Mission Statement be enlarged to encourage commitment to other programs and services not

Butler, "Bridge-builder and Gentle Persuader"

distinctly related to chemical dependency? Were other chronic illnesses appropriate for Hazelden's services, and what about the potential of a massive thrust into the field of health promotion?

Under debate was whether Hazelden's quest for creativity as a pioneer and as a model of rehabilitative components had exhausted itself; whether Hazelden should expand the volume of its services to other chronic illnesses and beyond, while attempting to maintain the high quality for which it has such an excellent reputation.

The board was anxious about the same issue. As the variety of services increased, how would Hazelden safeguard their quality? A major reason for Hazelden's success as a role model in rehabilitation services was the effective employment of its Research and Evaluation Division to refine and improve the quality of Hazelden's rehabilitative efforts. These efforts at quality were further reinforced by the attention paid to licensure and accreditation regulations as well as to the quality assurance mechanisms strenuously pursued in the seventies.

On a practical level the question — should Hazelden expand the volume of its services beyond the realm of chemical dependency? — was being answered in opposing ways. In the late seventies the literature department's desire to publish material on subjects not directly related to A.A. and Al-Anon — for instance, compulsive overeating — was being curtailed, if only for a short interval. On the other hand, the Employee Assistance Program focused on many problems in addition to chemical dependency.

INTERNAL EXPANSION

In 1971 Hazelden had two major divisions: Administrative Services and Rehabilitation. Four more were added in 1978: Education and Consultation; Personnel; Research and Evaluation; and Training. By 1986 no fewer than nine divisions were in place: External Relations; Facilities and Operations; Fiscal Services; Human Resources; Planning and Evaluation; Professional Services; Rehabilitation; Training and Health Promotion; and Educational Materials.

By 1986 Educational Materials had replaced Rehabilitation as Hazelden's primary revenue producer, grossing half of Hazelden's revenue for that year. Rehabilitation was a close second with about 40 percent of the gross revenue, and Professional Services a distant third. Rapid and accelerated expansion demanded added revenues and better planning.

The Development Office, which consisted of one person in the late seventies, became a separate department with a staff of eight people and undertook a $12 million endowment campaign in the mid-eighties.

EXTERNAL EXPANSION

Two major building projects were undertaken in the seventies. The Butler Center, constructed in 1974, initially served as a center for research, literature, and administrative offices. The E. B. Osborn complex was completed in 1976 to house the Family Program, a continuing education center, and another rehabilitation unit (Cronin Hall).

More buildings were visible in the eighties:
- the Maintenance building (1980);
- the Renewal Center (1984);
- the Richmond Walker Center (1985);
- the Cork Center (1986);
- the Dietary Building (1987).

Off-campus sites multiplied. A partial listing includes the following:
- an outpatient program at St. Joseph's Hospital in St. Paul (1976);
- Hazelden Pioneer House in Plymouth, Minnesota for young people (1981);
- Clarence Snyder Hall in Turtle Lake, Wisconsin, a group home for adolescents (1982);
- Hazelden Lakeview, an outpatient program for a rural population in Alexandria, Minnesota;
- the Hazelden Park Avenue complex in Minneapolis for the Professional Services Division and the Women's Outpatient Program;
- Hanley-Hazelden in West Palm Beach, Florida, a rehabilitation and family services center (1986). The establishment of Hanley-Hazelden allowed Hazelden to think in terms of geographical regional divisions for the marketing and distribution of its services throughout the United States, and the likelihood of eventually locating an international office somewhere in Europe.

NEW SERVICES

Although some attempt at planning had been initiated during the seventies, it was not Hazelden's strongest point. In the late eighties, however, the Planning and Evaluation Division works closely with Fiscal Services and External Relations for strategic planning. Prior to the late eighties, Hazelden's eclectic and pragmatic philosophy prevented or governed its planning. Such a lack of planning was referred to as *the grazing principle.* In other words, Hazelden intuitively moved in those directions where it sensed that chemically dependent people needed help. To some, this deficiency in planning appeared to be a weakness, and yet out of it emerged great strength. In the seventies it was difficult to plan creatively because chemical dependency was a new and open field. Nevertheless, the grazing principle allowed the Rehabilitation Division to create new services and respond to a number of underserved populations in the field of chemical dependency.

Underserved Populations

Programs for young people and women were opened and became successful operational models.

Together, adolescents and young adults formed an underserved population in the seventies. In 1980 the Hazelden Board of Trustees committed itself to serving this group of people. In 1981 New Pioneer House (an extension of the Pioneer House founded by Pat Cronin in 1948) was acquired for this purpose. Adolescents and young adults were given the opportunity for recovery in the same dignified setting. Pioneer House has received a great deal of applause and attention for its skillful handling of this population. Professionals from many states and some countries have sought guidance from Hazelden Pioneer House for the treatment of young people.

During the first half of the eighties, the issues of adolescent chemical dependency — assessment, appropriate placement, and treatment — came under intense state and national scrutiny as a result of state and federal legislation to protect young people from abusive legal systems. In response to this, Hazelden endorsed, encouraged, and actively participated as a member of a Consortium of Minnesota Adolescent Treatment Centers, which created a major assessment and diagnostic tool unique to the adolescent population.

The Women's Resource Center, located at Hazelden's Park Avenue complex in Minneapolis, provides assessment and treatment components that allow for a secure, nurturing environment in which women learn to support each other, form bonds of trust, develop feelings of self-worth, and explore new alternatives in sobriety — all in an outpatient setting. One alumna of the program wrote to the Women's Resource Center, expressing her appreciation:

Your enthusiasm — your care — was what I needed and, thanks to God, I found you wonderful people and your program. I'm on the road to recovery and it feels good to believe in myself and feel so strong again.

Family Program

Beginning in the early sixties at Dia Linn in White Bear Lake, it became a custom for counselors to call members of patients' families in for conferences. This tradition was reinforced at Center City in 1966 when Dan Anderson took full charge and Harold Swift was hired. Family services were, however, at that time limited to conferences, telephone and letter contact, individual family counseling, and the distribution of therapeutic literature.

The inspiration for family participation in the treatment process was the Al-Anon Family Group movement that evolved into a unified fellowship in 1950. According to *Al-Anon's Twelve Steps and Twelve Traditions:* "It all began with the wives of early A.A. members who realized their own need for change."

The Hazelden Family Program was established in 1972. As a three-day workshop that met once a month, it was called the Spouse Program because it was assumed that the significant other had to be either a wife or husband. There were special groups for women, others for men. Soon the program was offered once a week for mixed groups, and then twice a week when the Family Services Department was moved to the E. B. Osborn complex in 1976. Later on, the Family Program implemented Rehabilitation's model of accepting new people every day of the year. People are presently encouraged to come for seven days.

Taking its lead from Al-Anon, the Family Program attempts to address the needs of patients' families with a modified version of the program chemically dependent people participate in at Hazelden. They are provided with information about chemical dependency as an illness, thereby helping them to realize that they have not caused the problem. Hazelden follows the Al-Anon approach in describing chemical dependency as a no-fault illness in which everyone is involved. It is not accurate to describe chemical dependency as the fault of a chemically dependent person affecting a group of victims. The struggle of chemically dependent people and of the people who love them is a struggle for spiritual, emotional survival. It is difficult to find fault in this kind of situation, as A.A. and Al-Anon members come to realize.

Participants in the Family Program are presented with ideas about how to improve the quality of their family lives. The pro-

The Renewal Center   *Cork Center*

gram relies heavily on the interaction of the peer group — or one Al-Anon member talking to another over a cup of coffee. The Family Program's quiet, inspiring, creative, and simple method has received attention and imitation from professionals everywhere; the program's prestige derives from the unassuming manner in which it seeks to assist families and significant others through persistent, respectful presentation of Al-Anon principles. In this regard, the permanent part of the Hazelden model is its strict adherence to the program, process, and principles of A.A. and Al-Anon and other Twelve Step organizations.

One woman who, with her husband, participated in the program said:

> We have shared two years of sobriety and serenity and we are *grateful* for the *gift* we received from Hazelden.

Renewal Center

Another unique service that Hazelden created was the Renewal Center — intended as a haven for continuing personal and spiritual renewal. If primary rehabilitation is symbolic of the beginning of a journey toward recovery, the Renewal Center is a symbol of ongoing recovery. It provides an atmosphere of relaxed hospitality as well as time and serenity for continuing the journey of recovery. The Renewal Center becomes a place where people in recovery can meet, share their lives, be gracious to one another, and be renewed; its quiet, contemplative setting allows time for formal and informal discussions as well as for solitary thought.

Many of Hazelden's former clients have joined together through a bond of unique experience to actively support Hazelden's mission. One member spoke for many of those who belong to the alumni association, in saying:

> Many of us have been granted the gift of life itself, and we are grateful each in our own way.

Supported mostly through alumni efforts and gifts, the Renewal Center is a special example of this gratitude. As one alumni on his spiritual odyssey observed:

> The Renewal Center is like the A.A. program. From the front, the building seems like it's small, with a narrow opening. When you get inside, however, you see how large and comfortable it really is. When you go all the way through, and look back upon it — it seems awesome.

Professional Services

The division of Professional Services includes Training, Continuing Education, and the Employee Assistance Program. Training and Continuing Education were originally intended to inform others about the illness of chemical dependency and the recovery process so that others could help those in need.

The Employee Assistance Program (EAP) reaches out to a very large population — not only to those suffering from chemical dependency, but to employees and their families who encounter other problems as well. Pat Butler's ideas in the early fifties about employee assistance took hold in 1976 when a small department was established to deal with many requests from employers for employee assistance. Today Hazelden's Employee Assistance Services provide counseling services to 75 organizations (including corporations and government agencies) and to over half a million people nationwide. The department coordinates a nationwide network of approved, independent counseling services and treatment centers. Assistance is provided in person, or 24 hours a day, every day of the year over the phone.

The program has had a solid success rate and has helped employers by improving the job performance of valued employees, by salvaging employees who at one time might have been fired, and by protecting a company's investment in employee training. But the financial bottom line is only half of the reason employers use Hazelden's EAP; companies that offer the EAP as a benefit to employees consider their employees' health, productivity, and quality of life to be important concerns.

Employee assistance is another form of Hazelden's graciousness. The problems that touch people's lives at work and at home can be resolved; employee assistance opens avenues to help people regain their energy, stamina, and creativity.

Educational Materials

While Hazelden was a pioneer in developing a rehabilitation model, it was also a pioneer in becoming the world's largest publisher of chemical dependency, addictive behavior, and self-help literature. The Hazelden Educational Materials catalog contains more than 1,400 titles — books, films, audio and video cassettes, and pamphlets.

Hazelden's publishing component can be thought of as having a twofold purpose.

• Nourishing and nurturing the recovering and nonrecovering alike.

• Educating professionals and nonprofessionals.

Hazelden publishes meditation books to provide daily sustenance for everyone's spiritual odyssey, reemphasizing Hazelden's commitment to the spiritual dimension of recovery. Its classic best-seller, *Twenty-Four Hours a Day*, affectionately known throughout the world as "The Little Black Book," has sold over four million copies. The expansion of Hazelden's mission and its outreach to more and more people — families and friends of chemically dependent people, adult children of alcoholics and dysfunctional families, eating disorder sufferers, and those with chronic illness — is clearly reflected in the publication of its meditation books, which appeal to a broad range of people.

As one reader wrote:

> Your meditation books have enhanced and enriched my journey through life and assisted me in accepting the changes that have continued my growth. Thank-you.

The Cork Center

The Cork Center is the embodiment of Hazelden's emphasis on health promotion and wellness. The Cork complex includes rooms for educational services and workshops, as well as a Nautilus Room, swimming pool, basketball and volleyball court, an elevated running track, and other opportunities for exercise. Hazelden's future will emphasize health promotion and helping people live with chronic conditions of all kinds. According to Dan Anderson, Hazelden's future goal is to help improve the lifestyle of anyone who comes in contact with Hazelden, and to not only help prevent chronic disease in young people, but to teach people of all ages to change their lives in positive ways.

Some board members, staff, and alumni were apprehensive of the expansion and the building programs in the sixties, wondering whether the larger numbers and institutionalization would fatally damage whatever was in the little black box that helped people recover. In the eighties, similar expressions of fear were heard in regard to Hazelden's apparent attempt to become all things to all men and women. It may be, however, that the eighties are simply a continuation of Hazelden's very effective grazing philosophy and the application of the principle of graciousness.

In the Introduction to this book, I wrote that graciousness is what Hazelden is all about, that Hazelden graces people in many ways. Those who enter Hazelden's doors come from various backgrounds, but share the same needs — the need to understand, the need to express, and the need to share with others their human dignity, grace, and spirituality, which Hazelden, through its beautiful environment and caring staff, helps them achieve.

The ongoing history of Hazelden is the history of the many people who have entered its doors. They endured one of life's many crucibles and found the knowledge, the serenity, and the wisdom necessary to chart the sometimes stormy, but always rewarding course of a *continuing spiritual odyssey.*

Select Bibliography

ALTHOUGH *HAZELDEN — A SPIRITUAL ODYSSEY* deals with history, not every available source has been utilized. Every source that has been utilized has not been historically tested, particularly the numerous private interviews where time has taken its toll on personal memories and recollections.

Due to the style in which I chose to write this book, I decided not to burden the reader with hundreds of footnotes and a thorough analysis of all sources employed. I am able to point to a reliable source to validate everything I have written within these pages. I am willing to oblige any reader who wishes to pursue further anything written herein.

What follows is a list of some of the printed materials I used as sources of reference in writing *Hazelden — A Spiritual Odyssey.*

Anderson, Daniel J. *Perspectives on Treatment — The Minnesota Experience.* Center City, Minn.: Hazelden Educational Materials, 1981.

Bjorklund, Paul. *What is Spirituality?* Center City, Minn.: Hazelden Educational Materials, 1983.

Booth, Rev. Leo. "Principles Not Preachments." *Alcoholism/The National Magazine* vol. 3, no. 2 (1982): 62

Dollard, Jerry. *Toward Spirituality: The Inner Journey.* Center City, Minn.: Hazelden Educational Materials, 1983.

Kurtz, Ernest. *Not God, A History of Alcoholics Anonymous.* Center City, Minn.: Hazelden Educational Materials, 1979.

Select Bibliography

Laundergan, J. Clark. *Easy Does It.* Center City, Minn.: Hazelden Educational Materials, 1982.

Maxwell, Milton A. *The A.A. Experience.* New York: McGraw-Hill, 1984.

Richeson, Rev. Forrest. *Courage to Change.* Minneapolis: M&M Printing, 1978.

"Salute to Minnesota." *Alcoholism/The National Magazine* vol. 3, no. 2 (1982): 34-39.

Valliant, George E. *The Natural History of Alcoholism.* Cambridge: Harvard University Press, 1983.

THE TWELVE STEPS OF A.A.[*]

1. We admitted we were powerless over alcohol — that our lives had become unmanageable.

2. Came to believe that a Power greater than ourselves could restore us to sanity.

3. Made a decision to turn our will and our lives over to the care of God *as we understood Him.*

4. Made a searching and fearless moral inventory of ourselves.

5. Admitted to God, to ourselves, and to another human being the exact nature of our wrongs.

6. Were entirely ready to have God remove all these defects of character.

7. Humbly asked Him to remove our shortcomings.

8. Made a list of all persons we had harmed, and became willing to make amends to them all.

9. Made direct amends to such people wherever possible, except when to do so would injure them or others.

10. Continued to take personal inventory and when we were wrong promptly admitted it.

11. Sought through prayer and meditation to improve our conscious contact with God *as we understood Him,* praying only for knowledge of His will for us and the power to carry that out.

12. Having had a spiritual awakening as the result of these steps, we tried to carry this message to alcoholics, and to practice these principles in all our affairs.

---

*The Twelve Steps are taken from *Alcoholics Anonymous,* published by A.A. World Services, Inc., New York, NY, pp. 59-60. Reprinted with permission.

Index

Al-Anon, 7, 134, 161-162

Albrecht, Dr. Harold, 44-45

Alcoholics Anonymous, SEE: BIG BOOK

Alcoholics Anonymous, 12, 13, 16, 17-19, 31, 39, 47, 48, 72-74, 76, 77, 83
  Chicago fellowship, 11
  Dr. Bob, 14, 39, 47, 48
  in Hazelden, 7, 8, 85, 97, 130, 131, 143-145
  Higher Power, 18
  Oxford Group, 18-19
  spiritual program, 150-154 SEE: SPIRITUALITY
  term, "chemical dependency," 112
  Twenty-Four Hours a Day, 90-91
  "2218" clubhouse, 12, 28, 62, 73, 80, 83, 100, 112
  Bill W., 14, 17, 18, 25, 39, 47, 121, 152, 154
  and women alcoholics, 112

Alcoholism,
  adolescents, SEE: PIONEER HOUSE
  attitudes toward, 19, 47-48, 70
  recognition as disease, 47

  recovering alcoholics as counselors, 74-77, 85
  term, "chemical dependency," 112
  and women, Chapter 9 (107-115) SEE: DIA LINN

Alumni, 97, 99, 113, 162-163
  Center City Alumni Association, 99

"Amen" corner, 44

Anderson, Dan, 34, 70, 72, 75, 76, 77-78, 82, 84, 85, 86, 101, 102-104, 113, 114, 115, 118, 122-126, 128, 130, 131, 133-134, 135, 136, 138, 139, 147, 150, 161, 164, 169

Anderson, Elmer, 74

Arnold, John B., 86

Bacon, Selden, 85

Bailey, Bill, 123-124

Bibliotherapy, 7, 145 SEE: HAZELDEN EDUCATIONAL MATERIALS

Big Book, 7, 11, 39, 73, 136, 151, 153

Bigelow Auditorium, 138-139, 143

Bill W., SEE: ALCOHOLICS ANONYMOUS

Booth, Father Leo, 151, 169

Borden, Dorothy, 109
Bradley, Nelson, 34, 59, 62, 68, 69, 70, 71, 72, 73, 74, 75, 78, 80, 83, 84, 85, 111-112
Brandes, Mel, 73, 75
Briggs, Dr. Tom, 114
Brown, Phoebe, 109
Burke, Chet, 41, 44, 45
Burns, Bob, 125
Butler, Aimee Mott, 57, 63, 66, 91
Butler Center, 159
Butler, Emmett, 53, 54, 55, 98
Butler Family, 33, 45, 53-57, 60, 86, 96
Butler, Lawrence, 53, 54, 55
Butler, Patrick, 33, 40, 41, 43, 50, 52, 54, 55, 56, 57, 59, 60, 62, 66, 73, 80, 82, 84, 85, 86, 87, 90, 91, 100, 104, 108, 109, 113, 115, 118, 144, 146, 156, 157, 163
Cain, Jane, 112
Carlson, Archie F., 86
Carroll, Lynn, 12, 13, 14, 15, 16, 17, 20, 24, 27-29, 30, 31, 32, 33, 35, 36, 37, 39, 40, 41, 42, 44, 51, 52, 54, 55, 56, 73, 83, 84, 88, 89, 93, 96-97, 99-100, 101, 102, 103, 104-105, 108, 115, 118, 122-126, 129, 136, 146
  A.A. proponent, 29, 31
  resistance to Hazelden Model, 31, 104, 118-119, 126
Catholic church, 17-20
Center City, 6, 15
Cook, John, 61, 62, 63, 87
Cork Center, 6, 8, 159, 162, 164
Coyle Foundation, 24, 25, 51, 52, 53, 54
Cronin, B. Patrick (Pat), 11, 12, 43, 73, 83
Cronin Hall, 159
Crowe, Dan, 77
Curtin, Father, 60

Cushing, Archbishop Richard, 14
Dauw, Al, 123, 138
Dia Linn, 2, 84, 86, 102, 104, 106, Chapter 9 (107-115), 121, 123, 125, 130, 138, 143, 149, 161
  construction, 117-118
  Doll House, 110, 111
  extended care for men, 133
  Gate House, 110, 111
  multidisciplinary approach, 114
  reestablishment at Center City, 109, 115
Dowling, Father Edward, 17-18, 19
Educational Materials, SEE: HAZELDEN EDUCATIONAL MATERIALS
Eiden, Fred, 71, 72-73, 74, 75, 76, 85
Finn, Father Nicholas, 113
Fellowship Club, 58, Chapter 5 (59-67), 84, 86, 87, 104, 108, 117, 123, 143
  aftercare resources, 65
  halfway house concept, 59, 60, 66, 67, 117
  membership requirements, 61
  neighborhood opposition to, 60-61
  relocation, 64-65
  women admitted, 59
Frederickson, Dick, 125
Ford, Father John, 19
Fourré, Daniel, 119
Gordon, Bud MacCallister, 63
Grimm, Rev. Gordon, 79, 123, 125, 130, 134, 135, 136, 137, 147
"Guest House," 16, 17, 27, 89
Haas, Father Vincent, 19, 48
Halfway house concept, 59, 60, 66, 67, 117 SEE: FELLOWSHIP CLUB
Hanley-Hazelden, 159

Harkness, John, 114-115, 123, 124
Hazelden
  advertising, 86-87
  Al-Anon, 134, 161-162
  A.A., SEE: ALCOHOLICS
    ANONYMOUS, in Hazelden
  campus, 15, 22, 92, 93-94, 116,
    121, 139, 142
  clergy, 17-18, 19, 113, 137-138,
    150-151 SEE: SPIRITUALITY
  construction, 98-100, 113-114,
    117-122, 159
  counseling, SEE: HAZELDEN,
    training component
  Development Office, 158-159
  education and prevention, 86-
    91, 146, 159 SEE: HAZELDEN
    EDUCATIONAL
    MATERIALS
  employee assistance program,
    86-87, 158, 163-164
  evaluation and research, 32-33,
    35-36, 56, 131, 135-136, 158
  extended care, 129, 133
  family programs, 114-115, 129,
    134, 143, 159, 161-162
  Fifth Step, 46, 113, 151
  financial struggle in early
    years, 51-55
  health promotion, 158
  incorporation, not-for-profit, 24
  Information and Referral
    Center, 86, 87
  length of stay, 33, 97-98
  medical treatment, 40, 44, 48,
    103, 114, 125, 133-134, 143
  mission statement, 146, 157-158
  multidisciplinary model, 31, 34,
    36, 102-105, 114-115, Chapter
    11 (129-140) SEE:
    MINNESOTA MODEL
  name origin, 26-27
  planning and evaluation, SEE:

  HAZELDEN, evaluation and
    research
  recreation, 45, 94, 164
  repeaters, 129, 132-133
  resistance to multidisciplinary
    model, 31, 104
  training component, 8, 36, 80,
    130, 136-138, 143, 146, 163-164
  Treatment Committee, 130, 131
  Twelve Step lectures, 39, 46, 74,
    102, 104
  Willmar experience in
    Hazelden, 103-104
  women, SEE: DIA LINN
Hazelden Educational Materials,
  5, 6, 7, 89-91, 102, 129, 138, 158,
  164 SEE: *TWENTY-FOUR
  HOURS A DAY*; RICHMOND
  WALKER
Hazelden Lakeview, 159
Hazelden Model, 80, 102-105,
  108, Chapter 11 (129-140), 144-
  147, 157 SEE: MINNESOTA
  MODEL
Hazelden Newsletter, 87-88
Hazelden Park Avenue, 159
Heckman, A. A., 24, 32, 33-37,
  55, 135
Heilman, Dr. Richard, 125, 134
"Hidden Man, The," 88
Hill Foundation, SEE:
  LEXINGTON-HILL
  FOUNDATION
Hill Grant, SEE: LEXINGTON-
  HILL GRANT
Hill, Louis W., 33, 34
Hopponen, J. C., 86
Ignatia Hall, 122, 125, 133-134,
  140, 143
Ignatia, Sister, 48
Inspiration for Recovery, 52, 89
Jackson, John, 74
Jacobson, Lon, 44, 87-88, 89, 100,

101, 113, 123-124, 136
Jellinek, Dr. E. M., 71, 88, 139
Jellinek Hall, 139, 143
Johnson, Rev. Vern, 113
Kaiser, Frank, 62
Kauffmann, Rev. John, 78
Keller, Rev. John, 76, 79, 113
Kelley, Dave, 101
Kerwin, Jack, 13, 15, 16, 24, 51
Kroc, Joan, 8
Kurtz, Ernest, 18, 44, 47, 48, 169
Larson, Orv, 66, 67, 117
Lennon, Jim, 86
Lexington-Hill Foundation, 36
Lexington-Hill Grant, 33, 34, 35, 53
Lilly Hall, 23, 139, 143
Lilly, Richard Coyle, 14, 15, 16, 17, 23-24, 27, 28, 33, 34, 35, 37, 51, 52, 53, 54, 55, 139-140 SEE: COYLE FOUNDATION
Lindstrom, 15
M., Father, 11, 12, 13, 28
McGarvey, Robert, 13, 14, 15, 16, 17, 24, 25, 28, 51, 52, 53, 55
McGee, Bill, 78
McGoorty, Bob, 118
Maier, T. D., 24, 53
Malm, James, 30, 94, 138
Mann, Marty, 112
Maxwell, Lowell, 74
Maxwell, Milton, 151-152
Mehrer, Al, 125
Mill, Bill, 101
Mill, Jane, 109, 110, 123
Minnesota Model, 69, 71, 76, Chapter 11 (129-140)
  clergy, 78-80, 137
  family issues, 114-115, 129, 134-135
  multidisciplinary approach developed, 34, 72, 74-76, 102-104, 114-115, 130, 144-147

recovering alcoholics as counselors, 74-77
relationship with A.A., 72-74
Twelve Step lectures, 73, 102
SEE: NELSON BRADLEY; WILLMAR STATE HOSPITAL; HAZELDEN MODEL
Moos, Malcolm, 139-140
Multidisciplinary approach, SEE: MINNESOTA MODEL; HAZELDEN MODEL
Murphy, Leroy "Bud," 86-87
Murray, Archbishop John G., 12, 13, 15, 16, 17, 18, 19-20, 24
Nienaber, George, 60, 108
"Nightmare alley," 98
O'Brien, Earl J., 86
Old Lodge, 6, 26, 43, 94, 95, 96, 99, 102, 118-119, 123, 125, 126, 132, 143, 149
  and experimentation, 132
Osborn Complex, the E. B., 159, 161
O'Shaughnessy, I. A., 14, 15, 16, 17, 52
Otis, James, 88
Paddock, Richard, 123-124
Peterson, Hal J., 138
Pine Cottage, 133
Pioneer House, 36, 73, 78, 80, 83, 160
Poor, Lucille, 78
Porter, Andrew, 26
Power, Charles, 26-27
Power, Charles Jr., 27
Power Farm, 15-16, 24, 26-27, 30, 51
Power, Hazel Thompson, 26-27
Publishing, SEE: HAZELDEN EDUCATIONAL MATERIALS
Rehabilitation, 129-134, Chapter 12 (143-147), 158
Relapse, SEE: HAZELDEN, repeaters

Renewal Center, 6, 7, 159, 162-163

Richeson, Rev. Forrest, 78, 88

Ridder, B. H., 16, 17

Ripley, Austin, 12, 13, 14, 15, 16, 17, 20, 24, 25, 51

Rossen, Ralph, 71

Rossi, Jean, 72, 76

Schnable, Ann, "Ma," 29-30, 40, 42, 101

Schneider, R. Michael, 119

Shoemaker Hall, 121, 138, 143

Shoemaker, Rev. Dr. Samuel, 121

Silkworth Hall, 143

Silkworth, Dr. William Duncan, 120-121

Smith, Dr. Bob, SEE: ALCOHOLICS ANONY- MOUS, Dr. Bob

Smith Dee, 125, 134

"Snake pit," 70, 71, 98

Snyder Hall (Clarence Snyder Hall), 159

Solberg, Dick, 118, 123, 124-125, 130, 132, 135, 136, 147

Spirituality, 143, Chapter 13 (149-154)

"Squirrel cage," 98

Steele, Glen, 73

Stein, Reggie, 125

Sullivan, Tim, 118

Swift, Harold, 125, 130, 134-135, 136, 147, 161

Taylor, Bob, 100

Taylor, Hazel, 109

Tiebout Hall, 143

Tiebout, Harry M., 120-121

Triemant, Nick, 94

Twenty-Four Hours a Day, 90-91, 117, 138, 164

"2218" clubhouse, SEE: ALCOHOLICS ANONYMOUS

Walker, Richmond, 90-91

Richmond Walker Center, 6, 7, 159

Ward, Charles, A., 52, 53

Washburn, W. O., 108

Wegner, Marwood, 133-134

Willmar State Hospital, 12, 34, 36, 55, 59, Chapter 6 (69-80), 83, 84, 97, 102, 103, 104, 111, 114, 125, 134, 135, 137

and A.A., 76, 77, 78, 79

aftercare, 78

annual workshops, 73

clergy, 78-80

counselor training, 80

lecture series, 74

multidisciplinary approach, SEE: MINNESOTA MODEL

recovering alcoholics as counselors, 73-77

research, 80

staff cooperation, 74-77

Wilson, Bill, SEE: ALCOHOLICS ANONYMOUS, Bill W.

Winzerling, Father Oscar, 46, 78

Wojtowicz, Eugene, 123, 124, 125, 130, 131, 133, 136-137, 147, 150-151

Wold, Ted, 118

Yale Summer School of Alcohol Studies, 84, 102, 109

Zapp, Otto, 41-43, 44, 45, 46, 73, 86, 89, 100, 101, 136